A Kind of Splendor

A Kind of Splendor

Jacque Goettsche
and
Phyllis Prokop

BROADMAN PRESS
Nashville, Tennessee

Dewey Decimal Classification: 920
Subject Heading: WOMEN — BIOGRAPHY
Library of Congress Catalogue Number: 80-66025
Printed in the United States of America

DEDICATION

This book is dedicated with both love and respect
to all women
because we share
the glory of goals
the beauty of accomplishment
the vigor of decision
and
the appreciation of our unique gifts
which contribute to the world *A Kind of Splendor*.

ACKNOWLEDGMENT

We wish to express grateful appreciation to
Sandra Benson
and
Pamela McElwee
who have contributed constant help
and enjoyment to the writing of this book.

FOREWORD

We went into the writing of this book with curiosity and interest. We came out with respect and even a little awe. Our aim was to talk with outstanding women to discover the reasons for their success and their techniques for mastering their circumstances.

We found this, but we found something more. We found that Rosalynn Carter has a splendor of faith, that Liz Carpenter has a splendor of resilience, that Ann Campbell has a splendor of common sense, that Dale Evans Rogers has a splendor of devotion—in short, we found that each of these women who has faced great challenges has *A Kind of Splendor*.

JACQUE GOETTSCHE
PHYLLIS PROKOP

CONTENTS

First Lady Rosalynn Carter is a wife and a mother, as well as hostess of the most prestigious home in the world. She speaks of challenge, of strength, and of fun. These three words tell us much of her own individual approach to her position as respected companion and advisor to the President.

1. Rosalynn Carter

First Lady, Associate to the President, and Homemaker in the White House

"It's very much home upstairs in the White House, and I think that's important."

A visit with Rosalynn Carter is a visit home. There is a feeling of a back-porch get-together about the conversation, which is interrupted with frequent laughter. But no one will look into Rosalynn Carter's eyes without the realization that here is an able, determined, self-disciplined woman who has work to do after the visit is finished.

We had anticipated the interview with some of the stomach butterflies which seem to be a part of a visit to the White House. We had checked our list of questions and our tape recorder once again to be sure that all was in order. But when Press Secretary Mary Hoyt took us into the airy, yellow-toned office, and Mrs. Carter stepped up with extended hand, the butterflies stilled their wings, and an easy, relaxed atmosphere enveloped us.

We were first struck with how much prettier Mrs. Carter is in person than she is on the television screen. Her skin is more luminous, her manner softer, and there is a fragile aura about her which the camera does not capture.

She was dressed in a soft brown skirt, brown silk blouse, and brown pumps. Her make-up and nails matched the russet shades of her clothing with a pleasant dressed-with-care look.

She quietly got us settled on a yellow sofa with green stripes.

11

Then she sat facing us, ready to begin.

At the outset we wanted to know something of her spiritual life during the tightly scheduled and doubtlessly harried days as First Lady. Was there time for the Bible reading and prayers which we knew were a part of her life? She told us of the worship she shares with President Carter.

"Jimmy and I read the Bible together every night. We actually read after we get in bed. I read aloud one night and he reads the next. We read in Spanish because we both study Spanish, and it's helpful in learning the language, and it is so good to have that little period of worship together."

There are a number of Scriptures which are favorites, but she remembered particularly the words of the Twenty-third Psalm, "The Lord is my shepherd; I shall not want." She recalls, "I used to say this over and over in my mind when my children were growing up. If you know that the Lord is your shepherd and you know he's taking care of you, then everything else will work out all right. And then we had a Billy Graham movie in Americus, Georgia. The people came in and we were instructed on how to witness, and Jimmy headed up the effort in our area. We had workshops on witnessing so that at the end of the movie when people were invited to come up to the front we who had been in workshops could go down and witness to them. And I remember walking down that aisle in the theatre because I had never done anything like that and I said, "I can do all things through Christ who strengtheneth me" (Phil. 4:13). And the verse got to be very meaningful to me later because I've been thrown into so many situations that are overwhelming, and I can just remember that Scripture, about Christ strengthening us, and it's been a great source of help."

The challenging situation of becoming First Lady did not strike Mrs. Carter suddenly since she had been campaigning for so long, but there was for her that moment when she realized that it had really happened.

"When it actually happens it's overwhelming. And I think the greatest sense of change was that, all of a sudden, I knew it was my responsibility to follow through with these things I had been saying I wanted to do. It was my responsibility to do them now and not just talk about them. I don't exactly know how to express it, but it's an awesome responsibility, and you just assume that responsibility and you feel it. Immediately it seems I realized that we had won the election, and I had thought that we were going to win, but I didn't realize what a change it would be in the way I felt about it until Jimmy was elected."

To her the greatest excitement was when he decided to run and the idea was still new to her. Earlier, it had not occurred to her that he might run for the presidency and that she might actually become First Lady. That first realization that it was a possibility was the most exciting time. She cannot recall, however, the moment she first accepted the idea as a reality.

"He never did say 'I want to run for president.' I mean he didn't say that to me when he first started. We had people at home that would talk to him about it, old friends of ours. And so we started with the idea without Jimmy just thinking one day that he might run. It was an idea that people were talking about to us, but I don't even remember when he first said it. We've tried to think about it a lot of times to remember when we first started talking about it seriously, but I can't remember the first time that it was serious instead of just being a discussion. It just kind of worked into being a serious thing that we were considering."

It is apparent that the President and Mrs. Carter have shared their thoughts, plans, and ideas very closely through the years, and it is also apparent that she brings her share of personal strengths into the relationship.

She feels that it is important for people to feel secure in the family, to feel that they're loved, and she sees stability coming from a close relationship. She says with assurance, "The closeness with me and the family is very important to him. He is so busy and has such awesome responsibilities. So I think I give him strength. We try to have a normal family life in the White House, and I think we do.

"We have children coming in and out and back and forth. We've had three grand babies for a visit and they have just left. And it's very much home upstairs in the White House, and I think that's important. But really Jimmy and I have always worked together on becoming partners in whatever we did. Whatever I did he was interested in, and whatever he did I was interested in. And he's always encouraged me to do those things that I felt were important. For instance, when he was governor I had my projects that I was working on, and I always wanted to know what he was doing, and so we had a good, comfortable respect for each other's accomplishments."

We were surprised to learn that Mrs. Carter feels, in spite of her busy schedule, that she has had more time with her children since her husband has been governor and then president. She feels that she has given more thoughtful attention to them because earlier she had been a working mother, with the children constantly in and out of the house with their own distracting schedules. They were together as a family, but before the move to the Georgia mansion, they did not reserve the time for relaxed visits. In a sense they were together but too busy to share their thoughts.

She has analyzed the situation carefully and decided that when you are together all the time in that situation you don't plan special things. You don't plan to just sit down and visit and really enjoy being together, because you are always available.

"And," she said, "sometimes I think you lose a lot of contact with your children if they always go off to school and you are working. Now, I go with Amy every week to violin lessons, and I keep going because it takes twenty-five minutes to get there, and it takes twenty-five minutes to come home. We have really good conversations in the car, and then I practice with her every morning from 8 to 8:30. I think I make a point to do things that I would not do if I were home and we could be together all the time. But also when we were at home, Jimmy was campaigning a lot; we never saw each other. The boys were out campaigning or they were off in school. When he was elected governor all three boys were in college, and they all three came back to live in the governor's mansion. We had them at home in years when usually you don't have any children at home, so we really enjoyed this close family life."

Mrs. Carter also pointed out that life in the White House isolates its residents to an extent. Each member of the family feels the same responsibility to the public and this draws the family together. Also, it is difficult to get out. If they do go to a restaurant they will for security reasons be seated in a room apart. She sums up the situation, "So we stay at home." The children experience the same situation at school, so the family is pulled closer together and as she says, "We really enjoy being together as a family.

"I think it's very difficult when maybe teenagers or pre-teenagers are thrown into political life with a spotlight on them after having not been in it before. That would be a very difficult time, but my children were all in college, even when Jimmy was governor, and Amy was 3, so it's just kind of a way of life to her. She's never known anything else.

"We moved to Atlanta before a lot of attention was focused on the children. They had that time to become accustomed to criticisms which are a really difficult problem of children, particularly in school when other children are saying things about your father. And so my children have adjusted well to it. I was always real proud of them."

Mrs. Carter recalls the days in the Georgia mansion with pleasure. She feels that the mansion is one of the most beautiful in the country since it has columns on all four sides and is situated on an eighteen-acre fenced lot much like the White House. She describes the first floor furnishings as very similar to the White House. It is done with Federal period furniture, and the same decorating firm that decorated the White House did all the draperies and bedspreads.

She feels the pressures of the First Lady of Georgia were less than the ones at the White House, primarily because she did not have the concentrated attention of the press, and her schedule did not have to be given to the reporters. Also, the children did not have to have security to attend school, and this added relaxation.

The greatest change in coming to the White House is that every aspect of her life has attention focused on it. "Every aspect is so visible, so examined, and so dissected." Then with a chuckle she adds, "You get so you just expect it and you take it in stride."

We wondered if she had developed any protective mechanisms from the scrutiny by the press and public. She responded that the family being together in the situation is very relaxing and strengthening. Then she returned to the thought which is so much a part of her, "I think you have to have a strong faith; I don't know what we would do in this position without it. You have to feel that you're doing the best job you can possibly do and that you're not doing it alone because you have help from God."

The task of setting priorities as First Lady is not a light matter with Rosalynn Carter, and she feels that she could not have anticipated the broad range of people who would come for help. She is so aware that she is in a position to help. "There are so many people reaching out to you, you do have influence, and you can help in so many situations. This is why it is so difficult to set priorities. Sometimes it is just overwhelming."

That is the heavy side of her life, but the lighter side is that life with Jimmy Carter is to her "active, challenging, with never a dull moment."

There is a special time of day for her, a particular hour much like we remember from high school and college days, that time when the best date called with plans for doing something special. The President calls at 4:00 or 4:30 for her to go run with him or to play tennis. She runs two miles a day and he runs four or five. If the weather is bad and it is snowing, they go to the bowling alley downstairs. This time is special for her and she regards it as "really fun. I have done more physical exercise since Jimmy has been president than ever before."

With a sparkle in her eye she tells of trips to Camp David on weekends where they swim and do some cross-country skiing. They started jogging to get in shape for the cross-country skiing, and now it is a part of their schedule.

We gained a whole new view of the dignified drive to the White House as she said, "It's a quarter of a mile around this driveway on the south side of the lawn." We found it a little less awe-inspiring to arrive by a drive which was measured by a jogger's trotting feet, especially when those feet belonged to the First Family.

We gained another new view of life at the White House as she reminded us that, after all, "you live where you work, and you can't work all the time because you can't survive." We just hadn't thought of the White House in exactly those terms—the place where you work, and the place where you live. Certainly it is exactly that, but it takes Mrs. Carter's practical attitude to put it in that simple context.

The Carters not only read and study Spanish together, they also have through the years studied art and the great artists together. "Jimmy has always been interested in everything," she says. "He has always tried to broaden his scope of knowledge and his horizons. I remember once we had a friend at the radio station, and he would send us all the operas because he didn't have the radio audience for them. We got a book on opera and listened to opera and would read the story, so we've always done things like that."

As she talked, the reference to "fun" came up again and always it was with the little-girl quality which is so much a part of her personality. There was a feeling that the Carters carefully and consciously plan for fun to be a part of their lives, and they refuse to give it up even under the pressure of responsibilities. But soon Mrs. Carter returned to the topic of pressures. She feels that probably her mother had the greatest influence on her and helped her to develop the ability to cope in the presence of stress.

Her father died when Rosalynn was thirteen. She was the oldest of four children. Her mother had been an only child, and she wanted more children of her own since she had so much attention focused on her because of her only-child status. Mrs. Carter told us, "My father was nine years older than my mother and had always taken care of everything. Then he died, and in the next year her mother died. She was all of a sudden just alone, and I watched her go from a very protected person to a very strong person. She raised all four of the children, sent us all to college, and developed into a sturdy person who was always patient with us. She was just a really great person, and I think that from seeing her and having that influence on my life I was able to cope with situations."

We felt that we were hearing an explanation of the ability of our First Lady to deal with family, home, stress, and political criticism. She continued, "I could always think that if my mother can do it, then I can do it. You see, because anything that I faced was so minor compared to her losing a husband and her mother at the same time and raising four small children. She went to work in a grocery store, in the school lunch room, and then in the post office when I was still in school, and she just retired in 1975."

Mrs. Carter remembers with contentment the community of

Plains, Georgia, where she grew up. "I think growing up in a small town causes you to have a sense of belonging in a community and being secure, because in a community like Plains if anybody is sick everybody helps them. If anybody has a real problem, they try to help take care of it. And the communities are small and if you need a swimming pool, the people in the community band together to raise money and build a swimming pool.

"You have a sense of community and a sense of being necessary. I know that it's different in certain cities, but I also think there are communities in cities where you could have that same feeling, and that's one thing that I'm working on. I'm trying to get people to feel responsible in our communities. And I have the experience from coming from a small town that helps me to understand what can happen when people care for the community. Another thing that I think helped me coming from the small town is that there are never any secrets in Plains. So I've never had anything to hide; my life has always been an open book."

Mrs. Carter laughed with delight as she continued, "It's not like coming here and having a great secluded past because it would have been impossible to keep anything a secret in Plains."

College for Rosalynn Carter was two years at a junior college. She was at the point of deciding whether to go into interior decorating, since she was interested in furniture, or into teaching, which had been the field her mother had studied for; she decided instead to marry Jimmy Carter in July following her June graduation.

Later when she returned to Plains she studied accounting from textbooks loaned to her by a friend who was head of the accounting department of the vocational-technical school.

She plans for Amy's future education, but says after rearing three grown sons that you can't decide for children what they will be. Her only wish is that Amy will have the opportunity to do whatever she wants to do.

We asked for a prescription for the happy marriage that insures the 4:30 call each afternoon for her to go jog or play tennis with her husband of over thirty years. She insists that she has no prescription, but she does feel that you must share the things you are doing and have a good rapport about them.

She gives an example, "For instance, I have friends whose husbands were in politics, and they were not involved in each other's interests, and so the gap just forms if the husband or the wife has an interest that the other does not share at all. I think that could be disruptive. But if a husband and wife have interests—if they are similar or if they are different—if they share them, it's really very helpful. I don't have a prescription for a good marriage, but I know that I have never felt that my place was to do this and Jimmy's place was to do that. We've always just kind of shared the things that we had to do, and he's always encouraged me to do those things that I was interested in, so it has been a good relationship."

One of Mrs. Carter's interests is the ERA which she feels has so many misconceptions clustered about it. "I think that if we ever get past the misunderstanding, it is going to be because we find some kind of educational process and let people know what it can do— because I think people are afraid of change and there has been so much talk, so much distortion about what the Equal Rights Amendment will do, that they are afraid of it.

"Women are afraid of it because they think it's going to change their lives drastically. It's not going to change their life at all unless they want those changes, unless they need those changes. If they become widowed or if they all of a sudden find themselves in the situation of divorce, with questions about property ownership, those kinds of situations, then they can understand what the Equal Rights Amendment will mean to them.

"But if they don't want to change their life-style, if they want be a school teacher, a housewife, or whatever, the Equal Rights Amendment is not going to change that. And so I think that's the kind of feeling we have to get across to people. We're going to form a task force in the White House to bring people in from the states that have not ratified, where there is a chance to ratify. We can't just work with the legislators because before they can be for it, their constituents have to be for it. It's the same as on issues like the Panama Canal where there was so much misunderstanding. We started bringing people in from over the states just to explain the situation to them, and without exception they left knowing what we were doing and support- ing our position. And so I think we're going to have to bring people in who are effective to help us get the message across. Judy, my daughter-in-law, spends full time practically working on the Equal Rights Amendment, so I think we have some good things going."

We remarked that we had heard Judy spoken of highly and her mother-in-law agreed heartily. "Judy is really grand, and she has an approach that's good because she is a housewife and she has two little babies. She can identify with so many people, and she knows the importance of presenting it to the woman in a career too. For too long I think it's been identified with the radical element and that has turned a lot of people off. And we've got to let those people know that you don't have to be that radical-type woman to support the Equal Rights Amendment."

The White House is in many respects a showcase of the con- tribution of each First Lady. There are reminders of their in- terests and their areas of work. What, we wondered, did Mrs. Carter feel her unique contribution to the nation would be?

"Well, I have several areas of interest and one, of course, is mental health, and I've worked very hard on that. I hope that we can get a report of the President's Commission on Mental Health that will give direction for a decade.

"We studied for a year with the Commission about what we

have in the country, and what we need, and we have 117 recommendations, but all of them do not require legislation. A lot of them can be done just by working through the existing agencies."

Mrs. Carter personally took the 117 recommendations before Senator Edward Kennedy's health sub-committee and became the first wife of an incumbent president since Mrs. Roosevelt to testify before a congressional committee.

She emphatically evaluates the need, "For instance, there are unbelievable numbers of programs that affect the mentally afflicted. To bring some coordination to those and get the people together so that each agency can see what the other one is doing is so needed."

Mrs. Carter's view of the way to accomplish these tasks is clear. "I've been working with people in communities, trying to get them to assume responsibility for their programs. When you're in this position you realize that there will never be money enough from the government to solve the problems, and that's not the way to do it, anyway. If the problems are going to be solved, it's going to be on the local level by people who care. And so if I can encourage people in their communities to assume responsibility and reach out to solve those problems and help those people who need help, I want to do that. It's exciting and it's very difficult because how do you start? But we've been working on it and we have some good, exciting plans.

"We want to remove the stigma from the elderly and the mentally ill. The stigma is just the fact that people think when you're old you're finished, you're through, you're not much good anymore. For instance, my grandmother was a person who stayed home and took care of the babies. She shelled the peas and was relegated to being in the house and helpful, but looked on as kind of past the time when she was really contributing. But, of course, that's a contradiction. I'm a grandmother now, I don't feel like I've got to sit down and shell peas the rest of my life or tend to babies, and so the conception of what an older person can do or how an older person should spend the rest of their years is a real stigma today in our country."

Before we left we asked one final question. What does Mrs. Carter enjoy most these days, what does she look forward to? With another hearty laugh she told us, "I look forward to my 4:30 call. I am through with all of my appointments then, and you can't believe how much good it does to get out. It just clears the air for me and Jimmy too, to go out and walk around the yard in the spring and enjoy the fresh air and just get away from it. It's an escape and then we come back to work.

"The pressures are always with us, but we have so many good things in the White House. It's a really great experience. We have access to the finest minds. If I ever want help from anybody I can call the experts in the field, the finest talents. It doesn't matter who you ask to perform in the White House— they'll come. And it's just an exciting, very interesting life. It's always a challenge."

The words "challenge," "strength," and "fun" had been the three words we heard repeated again and again by Mrs. Carter. Even her favorite Scripture was an assurance of strength from God to meet challenge. We felt the words would be basic in her approach to life, whether she were living in Plains or Washington. There is the challenge responded to with strength, and after that there is the enjoyment, the fun.

We had more of a good visit than merely an interview. It was over and we left, stopping to stand and admire the view from the drive as we chatted with the guards at the gate. We took away a memory of a First Lady who is responsible and devoted to her work, but who has retained a little-girlness which permits her to giggle happily, and like any girl with an attentive admirer, wait for the phone to ring at 4:30.

Connie Hill is a musician, a teacher, and a lover of the arts. She has survived with dignity the murder of her husband, plastic surgeon Dr. John Hill, as well as the court trials which clustered around his short and eventful life. She has adapted to the publicity surrounding the publication of the book, Blood and Money, *as well as the projected movie, and she is making her own contribution to the life of her adopted city.*

2. Connie Hill

Heartbreak and Horror After The Bizarre Murder of Her Husband

"I think it was necessary to be so angry at first because it helped me accept the things I was so angry about. Those things really existed; they were not imaginary things — but to continue to be angry about them, no."

Murder, court trials, rumor, and intrigue: these are all a part of the history of the white mansion on Houston's Kirby Drive. But as Connie Hill, the third wife of murdered plastic surgeon Dr. John Hill, answered the door to us, all of these events seemed as unreal as half-remembered fiction.

We were suddenly enveloped in the graciousness of our hostess's blue eyes and open, welcoming manner. She ushered us into the library off the living room, but it was impossible for us not to glance at the raised floor of the entry hall where we knew the bleeding, dying form of Doctor John Hill had lain on the night of September 24, 1972.

There is so much to remember as Connie begins to speak, but she recalls events with calmness and even a certain detachment. There is no hint of tears. She seems to refuse to enter again into the emotions of the 1971 mistrial verdict at the close of the trial in which he was accused of the murder of his wife, Joan Robinson Hill.

She has made her peace with her husband's murder in 1972 followed by the lengthy 1974 murder trial of those accused of links with that case. Beyond that, there was the civil trial involving her step-son Robert and his grandfather, Ash Robinson, in the attempt to settle the ownership of the Kirby Drive home. And sandwiched in among these were the ten million dollar slander suit filed against Ash Robinson by Dr. John Hill and the wrongful death suit against Ash Robinson for the death of Dr. John Hill.

It seems to be more than one young woman could survive. But Connie is surviving and more—she is living with a quiet dignity and expectancy for the future. What is the secret of her survival? Is it a faith? Is it an understanding deep within her? Is it some training from her childhood?

Perhaps it is all of these which enable her to say, "I certainly have no hatred. I have fear because I've lived through something that is terrifying, and I will probably always have a fear of walking into my home and wondering what is waiting for me. That's something I know I have to live with. But as far as being directly afraid that anyone will harm me, I don't think so. I have no feelings about the whole matter because if I allowed myself to hate, I think that would destroy me. I don't want to spend my energies hating someone, and so for me it is better to wipe it out, and that's what I have tried most to do. I don't want to take evil into my life.

"I never knew Joan Hill or Ash Robinson. I don't know any of those people, although some live right here on this street. I do know that everything that happened was tragic. I can't tell you what it was, but I don't want it in my life. And I will not let any of it here in this house. I am so sorry that Robert cannot know his grandmother and that he cannot be with his grandfather, but I have to say that it is not totally my choice who he sees, because Robert has a decision in whether he does or does not see his grandfather, and it has been his decision, on his own. He has discussed it with other people and made his decision. He decided it was not what he wanted."

Connie described Robert's attachment to her as his mother by saying, "Very shortly after John and I were married, someone asked him who his family members were. He named John's family and he named my family. And I think that says it.

He really does feel that we are his family, and we are. I'm very sorry but I can't run the risk of the tragedy in Joan's life becoming a part of his life."

The circumstances leading up to the murder at the couple's front door in 1972, as John and Connie returned from Las Vegas, had been described day after day like a high-adventure serial on the front pages of newspapers across the nation. It was a bizarre story, and it was a story very hard to associate with the smiling young woman pouring our tea into fragile cups. She talked and laughed easily as she moved about in black slacks and a dark green shirt. She didn't shy away from the past; on the contrary, she seemed to welcome the opportunity to tell of the events, not as others had described them but as she had experienced them.

Connie entered Dr. John Hill's world in December, 1969. She was participating in a musicale where she had played the harpsicord and sung a Scarlatti cantata. At the close of the performance, she had been taken aside by a friend to meet the handsome plastic surgeon whose love of music was as deep as her own.

It was widely known by crime buffs that there were questions about the death of Joan Robinson Hill, but it was not until late spring that he was indicted by the grand jury for her murder.

But all of this was a foreign world to Connie.

As she said, "First of all, I came here from Vienna where I had lived for a year. And when I came here I taught college voice for a year, and I'm not really one to read murder and trial stories in the newspaper. I just don't read them. It wasn't until after I met him that someone said, 'Oh, there's some question about whether he had something to do with the death of his wife.' And then you know how stories go. I thought about it, but it wasn't constantly on my mind. I was immediately with him in groups of other people. And all those others were people I liked and enjoyed, and we all shared music together, and John most of all, and I just could not see where on earth something like that story could have any credence.

"Maybe I had too much faith in my own good judgment. I don't know, but there are people you are with, and you are at ease and you don't sense anything amiss. I didn't sense anything that was not quite right. I knew there were problems, but at that point I had not lived long enough to make a judgment, I guess. And I'm not sure that anybody has until they go through something like that.

"When we first fell in love I felt that the problem was just going to go away, and we both felt that there was no real legal case there. I suppose the whole story was just not a part of my thought. I didn't even relate to anything as violent as being intentionally unkind to someone, so how could I relate to this? That is all so remote from me, and I just thought this was the wildest tale I'd ever heard. And here was his son Robert, a sweet, darling little boy, and Mrs. Hill, John's mother, who certainly had opinions of her own, but who was to me at all times the loveliest, most charming woman I could imagine.

"And so these great tales that I heard never ceased to amaze me. In fact, even yesterday I was checking it out, because I keep thinking, was I fooled? You know, was I really fooled? Because I would hate to think that I went through all of that and was misled, and I'm not about to let myself be fooled. I would really be disappointed with myself if I just accepted everything at face value."

With deep honesty she continued, "I'm sure that there are people who are shocked at the questions that I ask now about John because it's important to me to know that I was not wrong.

"All I know is what was, and what was is that we had a marvelous, marvelous relationship, and whether it was a little contrived because of the situation, I don't know. But whatever it was, I wouldn't give it up for the world, and I'd go through it all again for those three years with John."

Even the most news-hungry reporter had never thrown the

slightest cloud on Connie and John's marriage, and Thomas Thompson's *Blood and Money* had described it in glowing terms. What was so unusual about their marriage?

"I have to say that our marriage was beauty in every, every facet. I used to think about it that way, and later I thought of it as a perfect circle. There are relationships that you have with various people in your life, but there's always a portion that isn't quite in place. But in the one period of time that I knew John, which was about three years, all parts of that circle were present. There was the companionship, the respect for him in his work, and his respect for me, sexually, just every way. The whole thing was there.

"There were other people I had been in love with, but there was never anybody else I had that kind of relationship with. I had dated a professor from a school where I went for quite some time. I had dated a lawyer for quite a period of time in Philadelphia. And I had quite a serious relationship with a man who was a professor at Columbia, and so John was certainly not the first person that I had fallen in love with. I think you can fall in love with a lot of different people, but to find somebody that you have a whole relationship with is rare."

Connie admits that the perfection of this rapport may have been heightened by the threat facing them. "Some of that relationship may have been our great need for each other. Remember that when you're fighting a battle outside your home, everyone comes together and you don't fight among yourselves. You may fight the world and everybody else, but you don't fight with each other. However, that isn't what was on my mind at the time. It was just that I had a tremendous admiration for him, and he for me, and it worked beautifully."

We mentioned that John's mother was reported to have commented (at the beautiful society wedding of John to Joan Robinson) that the marriage was a "mismatch."

We fantasized that if Connie and John had met prior to his meeting with Joan Robinson and second wife Ann Kurth, their lives would have run a smooth contributing course rather than the rocky road of trials and death.

Connie thought along with us, "It's a fantasy, of course, and how can we possibly say? John may not have been the person that he was had he not lived with Joan for that period of time. It is possible that you can live with someone who is perfectly charming and lovely, and yet it's wrong for you, and for him it was wrong, and for her it was wrong. And perhaps he would not have been the same person when I met him if he had not had that experience. I don't know. Maybe he, in his desperate attempt to say, 'I am a good man, I can be a good husband,' went out of his way to treat me beautifully in what was not a real situation. You see what I mean? There are so many if's. Who knows?"

We were reminded that Connie and John knew each other for only three years and were married for only fifteen months before his death. We wanted to know if the shortness of time contributed to the idyllic nature of their marriage.

Connie talked easily of that brief period. "It was a perfect segment of time. He was an extremely busy doctor, and at the time I was extremely busy doing my music school and singing. And we both had our own world we were very successful in, and the time we had together was really pure joy. Yes, it was short. Now I know that had we gotten to the point of making a lot of decisions together that we would have had disagreements. But it is really true that we never had an argument where one stamped out and slammed the door; it just never happened.

"We seemed to complement each other. We enjoyed many of the same things, and yet a lot of different things. I think it's important for the man to be good in areas where the wife isn't, and the wife should be good where the man isn't, because you may just duplicate your contribution if you've got too much of the same thing; for instance, knock on wood, I don't ever want to marry a musician for the reason that I am already so immersed in music that my life needs someone who can bring more to me, and hopefully I can bring something to him.

"John was so involved in the medical community, and he also was a tinkerer in everything. If you look around the room you'll see all kinds of books on antique America. It never ceased to amaze me the things that he has read. He had read all of the Will Durant books. He read all these books you see here, and he was tremendously knowledgeable in a variety of things. Of course, he was very interested in politics, and he was much to the right of where I stand. But at the same time, I respected what he had to say and why he said it."

She began to tell us of her late husband's background. "He was from a very small and a very unsophisticated town, and I had lived in New York. I had gone to Vienna, and I had lived in Philadelphia and Princeton. I had been exposed to the finest things and had become somewhat sophisticated. John had the ability to appreciate those things, but he was really engrossed in the playing of the piano and medicine.

"He loved beautiful things, but he didn't know how to put them together and make them beautiful around him. I don't know, I just think in general I was a more liberal person than he, and we had long talks about a more liberal way of thinking as opposed to a more conservative way, and I influenced him and he influenced me. I think because of my travels I brought a lot of exposure to him that he would have given anything to have, but he had not had time to experience."

"Another thing is that I was and am a very organized person. John was totally disorganized. Everything, I mean his papers, den, his bedroom, everything was like scrambled eggs all the time. Well, you know, I honestly think that was a part of all of this problem that took place. He was like the absent-minded professor. Anyone could walk off with half of the office and it wouldn't bother him. He was just taking care of his patients. He didn't care. It was too much bother to worry about that. Taxes? What taxes? That's irresponsible, and he was to the point of almost complete irresponsibility in those areas."

Connie spoke of his brilliance by saying that she thought his intellect was beyond measure, and then she added, "I don't say that boastfully. I just think it's true. I knew that both he and his brother had extremely high intellects. I don't know exactly where this came from. I never knew his father, so I can't tell you anything about him. His mother is very bright. She did not have a college education, but I doubt that there is a woman anywhere who knows more about the Bible and politics. She knows what is there, and she can quote you anything you want quoted, and tell you why and how, and the history of it. At nineteen this woman came from a small town in Illinois to a small town in Texas. Where did all this learning come from? The answer is, she decided that she wanted to learn and she's still learning. She's still studying.

"She went from one point to the next and she put John in a situation where he could grow. This was John's experience, and this is what he brought to our marriage."

We turned from the thought of the marriage to its abrupt ending and Connie's part in that ending. She and John had come from the airport to discover a threatening figure opening their own front door to them. The person had a strange green covering over his face. Connie had escaped by running to a neighbor's home, only to hear two shots ring out behind her.

We recognized that this was an event of a magnitude which most people will never be called on to face. We remembered so well Connie's face staring out from the front pages during those days, and we asked what had sustained her during the first unreal hours. We asked, "What enabled you to stand up, to walk through those days after John's murder?"

"I just would have to say my inner strength, whatever that is and wherever it came from, I don't know. But it was there. I remember thinking at some point along the way that this was like a play, and I know the play and I was acting a part. I thought, *I'm doing all these things, but it isn't real.* Yet at the same time I knew it was real. I read somewhere, maybe something about widows and how they get through the first few weeks after death, and I discovered that the ones who were previously very well-organized and independent ordinarily behave just as I did. I didn't cry for a long time. Now that to me sounds like I'm very hard-hearted. But that wasn't what struck me. I'm a performer, and my immediate response to something like that was that things have to go on; things have to take place and I must help with them.

"I was used to being a hostess, and I was used to seeing to John's needs and to Robert's needs and as I said, performing. No matter if you're ill with the flu or whatever else, you go out on the stage, and you do what you know has to be done, and this was, at that point, what I had to do. So again I can't say where the strength came from, but it was my inner strength from somewhere that just carried me through.

"I didn't allow myself to grieve. Months later someone had to tell me that it was alright to grieve. I sought the help of a psychiatrist, not because I felt that I couldn't handle everything. All I knew was that something very unusual had happened to my life, and that even though I was functioning well at that time I wasn't sure that I was going to be able to handle things that would come later. I didn't know what they would be. I just knew that I probably would need some guidance, and so I began talking with a woman psychiatrist. I went to her and in retrospect I know that she recognized I had not really accepted the fact that John was gone and that he had been killed. It took a long time before I was able to say, 'Alright now, I must allow myself to say that he is gone, and that this has happened and express it some way.'

"I probably would never have been able to admit to myself what had happened, except that somewhere in the conversation it came up that I had not visited the grave, and I didn't feel guilty because I hadn't. I just didn't want to see it. But I knew I had to start somewhere, and that was the easiest place to begin because it was tangible. It was something I could actually do. I could march myself out there and say that spot is where John is, and he's gone and I must accept it. So I went and I stayed for quite some time, cried, and came home.

"After that Robert would come home from school, and I would greet him at the door and I would cry. I'm sure that was probably good for him, too. He had cried more at the beginning, and at that point he became my strength. He probably felt that I needed him at that time, and he would sit with me and not say very much but he'd just be there.

"There are so many people who have come to me and said, 'Robert was so fortunate to have you. He could not have survived if it hadn't been for you.' What they don't know is that I could not have survived without him because there were days when I'm sure I would have stayed in bed the entire day; I would not have gotten up and fixed breakfast, lunch, and dinner had I not known I had this child and his life had to continue. He must go back to school; this was a horrible thing that happened to us, but we had to go on. If I hadn't had to act that part out for someone, I may not have acted it out for myself. So, he was a tremendous source of strength.

"The children at school were very kind to him. All the children came to the funeral, and a lot of their parents sent him flowers. I thought it was so wonderful that one of the teachers came by to see him when he was very embarrassed about going back to school, which I'm not at all surprised about. The teacher said that she had observed a fight on the playground at school, and the fight was over who was Robert's best friend. And that's all it took and Robert went back to school. I don't know whether it actually happened or not; whether it did or not doesn't matter—that's what she told Robert, and from that time Robert was just so much better."

Connie had told us of her postponement of grief and we wondered about her later response. We had heard so much recently about the states of grief, what for her followed her permission to grieve?

"For me, after the initial shock and grief there was anger. First of all, I have to say that a lot of anger was not justified, but it was there and I had to deal with it. I was angry with John for having become involved in this whole thing to begin with. Whether he had anything to do with it or not was not related to my emotion of anger. I was angry with him. I was angry with his mother. I was angry with her for raising him in a situation where he never had to deal with the kind of people who would do this kind of thing to him. I was angry with the church, and I was angry with the system of government here in Houston that could allow that kind of thing to happen. I resented Robert. Here was this child whom I loved as my own; I don't say that I didn't love him. I resented him. He was a responsibility. I just wanted everything out of my life. I was very angry at everybody, some for justified reasons, others for unjustified reasons. But I had to deal with it."

We asked, "What kept you from just packing your suitcase and leaving Houston?"

"I'm not sure. Probably Robert's need to be here, and there were just things that had to be done. John's office had to be closed; there were all kinds of legal things that had to be taken care of. Someone did say, 'Let's just pack up and go,' and I said, 'I can't do that. I run a music school and I've got to take care of John's responsibilities.' There were just things that had to be done and I did them."

Connie seemed to be thinking back carefully to her own actions at that time.

"I guess we act in the manner we have been taught to act, and as our experience has trained us to act. It's just like the night John was killed. It didn't occur to me that I should fall on the floor and cry and scream. It was a shock; it was like someone had hit me so hard that I was dazed, but the minute I could get up I didn't fall and get emotional. My immediate thought was, *You've got to take care of the situation.* I can remember trying to deal with things as best I could the night John was killed. That is the most vivid time.

"It's really strange. I could tell you almost everything I did that night, but the following day and about the next week are a blur. In fact, I have talked to police, and they told me things I did and I'd swear that I didn't do them. I have no memory of things a little later. They have a tape recording of me, and after they played the recording for me I remembered that conversation. I know that I knew those things I was saying on the tape, but I don't remember the taping. And yet I'm told that I went on and functioned, and that I was able to cope with whatever happened."

Why did she remain after she had cared for the details of closing John's practice and caring for legal matters? We saw how far the strands of such a disaster reach into the future as she said, "It's a very unfortunate legal tangle that we're still involved in. As you may know from the recent trial that this house is jointly owned by Robert and his grandfather. But beyond that there is another reason for staying; there is the music room. There's the fact that John built the music room, and it's a very special room, not because it has expensive chandeliers and expensive pianos, but because the room is really a work of art and it should be preserved. The music there is probably as perfect as you will hear anywhere in the world because of the acoustics. It was John's dream to make it acoustically perfect, and I would say that it's probably as close to that as any place there will ever be. It doesn't matter whether there are 125 people or two in the room, the sound encompasses you and it is glorious. That kind of experience happens so rarely. I use it generally for small concerts and maybe for ten to fifteen people with fine performers. We share it with artists I know personally and think are especially gifted. Because of this I really don't know what we would decide to do about the house even if the legal tangle were settled.

"Our situation has changed just in the last few months because now Robert is gone and for me to live alone in this house is going to be something that I have to experience and decide about. Do I want to be here by myself? I don't know. When Robert was here, I enjoyed it. He enjoyed it, and it was a pleasure. But whether I want to stay here by myself, I don't know.

"Robert is very proud of the music room. You see, the music room is the best of his father. Robert is very proud of that and rightly so. It's a very beautiful thing, and if he loses that he will have lost so much of his heritage. It's like things that pass down through your family. That is one of the outstanding things that Robert has of his mother and father, so it's even more important to him than it would be to a child who had his parents alive and who received furniture or jewels that were a part of his childhood.

"And then Robert has his own love of music. It's not as strong as mine, and it might have been much stronger had his father been alive, and he had not had so many problems to deal with. He had so much tragedy that it was difficult for him to concentrate in school. He tried so hard and in the end he was getting A's and B's. But the extra time and concentration it took for him to play the guitar and piano, which were the instruments he was involved with, he just couldn't manage. He needed time to rest and play. I don't know how he ever did a math course. I just can't imagine the concentration it took for him to do that with the amount of pressure he was under. So you can see, with a love of music and also the identification of the room with his parents, what the music room symbolized for him even beyond its beauty."

We had earlier toured the music room and we understood what Connie was saying. The gold-and-white ballroom expanse was breathtaking and affecting in a way few rooms in the most famous castles are experienced. There were the vaulted ceilings. There were the parquet floors, bare at the end where the ten-foot Bosendorfer piano sat and covered with Chinese carpet under the French Provincial settees, which were placed for listeners to be not only comfortable but enthralled.

There were the chandeliers of Baccarat crystal, the fireplace of carved marble, the panels of satin brocade which opened at a touch to reveal stacks of music and record albums. There were four miles of wiring and 108 speakers and a movie screen housed in its inconspicuous slot in the ceiling. It is a room of opulence and joy.

Connie, John, and Robert had shared this room, and we began to see the three of them in our mind's eye more as a family than as three distinct people caught up in a maelstrom of confusion. We wondered how Connie had adjusted to her sudden role as mother to Robert who was ten when she first met his father.

She explained, "Robert was twelve when his father died. But you see, I had three brothers, all of whom were younger than I, so I diapered, raised, fed, and baby sat when I was growing up, so I didn't feel inadequate to the job. I had also been a school teacher, which was helpful.

"I asked for help, though. I did see a psychiatrist, and I was given some guidance there. I sought help from a positive feeling that I knew I was in a very unusual situation and even if I did everything right it was still going to be difficult at times. My youngest brother was ten years younger than I, the next closest brother was nine years younger, and the next was five years younger so that provided lots of experience. I watched my parents take them through baseball and disciplining at all the levels. Even though at some points I was off at college, I would hear all the things that happened, and I knew what is was to raise three boys. In my own family I didn't have the direct responsibility, but I almost felt directly responsible. I don't know why, but as the oldest sister I almost felt like a parent to them.

"As far as Robert is concerned, when John was alive, he was a very attentive father. I know that doesn't wash with what a lot of people have said, but you have to remember that John was a very busy doctor. Even though he wasn't with Robert an awful lot, the time he was with Robert he made count. When John would come home and we'd hear the garage door start to open, it wouldn't matter where Robert was. He would run and make a mad dash for that door to get it opened. When it was open you would have thought that John had been gone for months because John would say, 'Oh, there's my little boy.' And he'd run across, and there would be this great big jump, the hugs, and the exchange of what had happened all day, and then we'd all sit down together. Also, John spent time with Robert building rockets and taking him out for weekends. He took him places by himself, and he also spanked him. Of course, we have had the usual little problems.

"I can't tell you how I used to hate making Robert go up to clean his bedroom. He had great problems over cleaning up the bedroom and working in the yard and, particularly, in this neighborhood. Robert would say, 'Well, my friends told me they came by today, and they wanted to know if I was being punished by working in the yard.' In River Oaks you do not do your own yard; that is just the way it is. And my brother was with us on Saturdays, and he and Robert worked in the yard. And I guess this is my family all over again."

We suggested that it may always be a problem to teach children responsibility in wealthy homes where chores are not a real necessity and Connie agreed.

"I think it's harder for you because it's much easier to say, 'Miss Sally, go up and clean his room'; then you don't have to fight. You know, it just needs doing, and it's done. But at the time he is learning that there's pleasure in work, and I think in the end that's where we all have to find joy. Hopefully, you can teach him that there's pleasure in the doing. Sometimes there is such a big brawl that no one is sure. I have to say that as time passed and he got into high school and a lot of his friends had parents who were allowing other people to do the work Robert was doing at home, he would come home and brag, 'You know, I do this and they have someone else do it.' Then I knew we were making progress. But up to that point I was not sure what progress really was being made."

Connie had been faced with the necessity for so many courses of action about Robert and about her own life, and each action had demanded decision. We discussed the need for decision and she seemed to feel that there was nothing unusual in her care of special needs, that it was a direct result of her early life and training.

"I grew up in a self-disiplined household. One of the earliest things I remember was that my father worked as an engineer during the war and was very busy, and mother was the director of the church choir and a chorus. I remember constantly going to rehearsals. I think that's probably where I began my music.

"I remember my father getting up in the morning and taking me with him when he ran. He always ran. I would run as far as I could with him, and then sit down by the side of the road, and it seemed like he ran for years before he came back. But I could always go with him. His time with me, always his time with me, with my dog showing me the squirrels—I remember that very, very much. Then after the war we moved to a small town near Seattle, which is where my mother's parents were. They were a minister and his wife, and so we were very much influenced by the church, not only through my mother's activities but through my grandparents. We were with aunts and uncles and cousins almost always, and if we were not with them we were at church functions. I always went to Sunday School, and I always went to what we called Christian Endeavor. I played the piano and did all of the things a young person does in the church, and I think I still have a ten-year badge for never having missed a Sunday in that Presbyterian church. My parents expected me to achieve and encouraged me, too.

"I don't think at that time I thought of it as 'expect.' I remember my father saying it doesn't matter whether you are a janitor or a chief doctor, you should be the best of whatever it is. He not only said that to me, but he demonstrated it by taking me out in the yard where we had rings and bars. He would show me how to do acrobatics on them. And I was not just going to do it—I had to do it right.

"We were always very busy and I still have to be involved or I'm not happy. I grew up occupied and participating. The music I heard at that point was on the radio. My father played classical music on the radio and my mother had records. I remember Lily Pons. Oh, would I mimic Lily Pons! I could sing just as high as she and that made me as good as she. Oh, dear. And from that I went into the orchestra and that broadened my knowledge so much. At that point I had been studying piano and I sang a little bit. But the interest in the cello opened up so much more to me.

"As the years passed my father kept opening more and more doors in so many areas such as travel and architecture. Mother was in the music world which was where I was strongest, but he kept bringing all the rest of the world to me."

Even remembering the tragedies Connie could say, "I feel like a happy person; I think I was a happy child. All of this early training had developed attitudes I suppose helped me when disaster came. I have to say that I turned to myself more than to anyone else for help."

Connie felt that there was simply no place else to go. She remembered that some people said that she must have had great faith in the church, but she says, "At that point I hated the church. I remember the minister and those people coming into the house the day after John died, and I knew they were doing the loving thing and the acceptable thing, but I was too hurt and angry inside. I'll never forget sitting there talking with them, trying to say what I wanted for the funeral—the memorial service, I wanted it called. And the minister saying, 'And let us now pray.' It took everything within me not to scream, 'I hate you, I want out of here.' At that point it was so close to when it had happened, and I kept saying to myself, 'I have done everything for the church. I have been a missionary in my own way. I have gone to church, I have been a good wife for John, I have taken care of his child's health. How dare God allow this to happen to me!'

"I was furious, and it took me about two or three months, or perhaps not even that long, to pick up the Bible and start to read again. I don't know if it was in reading again or if it was in just understanding in general that helped me to realize there was no reason I should be spared sorrow.

"We were in the middle of the Vietnam war with families being destroyed for absolutely no reason. Boys were being killed. Vietnam was everywhere. Whatever your feelings are about Vietnam, people were being destroyed needlessly and so many were suffering seeing others' pain. I began to regain some of what I really believed, which is that God is everywhere around us."

Many people say when we have great difficulty if we help someone else that this helps lift the burden. We asked Connie if she had experienced this.

"I found great strength in realizing other people's burdens and realizing that they had survived them. At that point there was so much publicity, and there was so much concern for me and for Robert, I think for awhile people didn't want to burden me with other people's cares. But you get them and that's why I mention Vietnam. It was right there in front of me in the newspapers. As time passed, I became very sympathetic, terribly sympathetic to other people's problems. I was never very outwardly emotional, but I would cry when I would hear of someone else's problem or unhappiness."

Connie's growth was apparent as she talked. She had weathered so much and could now look back thoughtfully. Why had it all happened? What did she now see as John's areas of personal vulnerability in the disaster?

"I think the thing that was the most charming about him was the thing that probably was his demise, and that was his great naïvete. He could be with so many people and enjoy them totally, absolutely totally, and they would enjoy him, but he was being taken in. He didn't realize what they were doing to use him, because he was just enjoying it. Everything was a new adventure to him. Everything was love and just a delight. Whenever people were with him they were at their best and he made them happy.

"Also, as I mentioned earlier, his disorderliness made him vulnerable to anything that required specific records. He was open and eager toward everyone and he trusted everyone. These characteristics were all destructive in the long run."

She thought of herself in the situation as she continued, "I suppose this disorderliness was particularly hard for me to understand since I am very orderly. I had kept the books and also acted as secretary for my music school in addition to giving concerts and working with some 200 students and fifteen or twenty symphony members who were teachers. From this you can see that order was very much a part of me."

We asked Connie about the present status of her school and found that she had closed it some years before. Her interest in music had gone on, though, as she worked with the opera in a volunteer capacity. For several years she had tried to get teenagers involved in attending performances. Later, as she came to believe children needed to be convinced of the validity and joy of the opera at a younger age, she worked with an educational program for elementary age children. It was directed toward an understanding of the function of a director, costume and lighting designers, and all the various parts which make up a finished performance.

And what lies ahead now that Robert is away and the memories have become, if not dim, at least manageable?

"A new field," Connie says. "I have my real-estate license, and I'm going to get a broker's license. I'm a worker and I'm on this treadmill that will not let me off, no matter where I am or what I'm doing."

Connie's eyes flash with enthusiasm, because obviously the treadmill is one of living and not one of drudgery. She thinks of the new experiences waiting and remarks on the pleasant trips to Aspen, Colorado, for lectures, and what she describes as the most beautiful music conference followed by tennis, hiking, and tailgate picnics in the mountains. With a faraway look she adds, "Someday I guess I want a person to share my life with, but at the same time I don't ever want to feel that if that person disappears from my life I will be totally lost."

We started to say goodbye and Connie added, "Tragedy is only comparative to what you've experienced before. So if the tragedy in your life is that you have a lame leg, that is a tremendous tragedy to you. And if it is the loss of a loved one, it can be that much more tragic. It may seem more tragic to those from the outside, but if it is your cross to bear, you have to deal with it with all the strength and dignity you have at your command."

We talked about little things before we left—the way the tones in a painting picked up the same tone in the sofa, the tinkling sound the harpsicord made to our unaccustomed hands, and the collection of recorders in the case at the side of the room.

It had been a good visit, but most of all it had been a touch with young, vibrant courage which said, "I refuse to hate; I refuse to brood. I will build a life of the good things that remain."

3. Liz Carpenter

Spokeswoman for Women,
Serving Her Country

"A very bright woman said to me shortly after Les died, 'You have to think of the rest of your life as your second life and not just what is left over. Think of it as starting for the second time, and don't do anything the way you did it before.'"

What do you do when your first life ends? You begin your second life. That's what Liz Carpenter, journalist and former press secretary to Lady Bird Johnson, learned when her thirty-two-year marriage suddenly ended with the death of Leslie Carpenter.

"Grass Roots" is the name of the home where Liz Carpenter is living her second life. The house is fitted into the side of a rocky hill, and it is approached by a road which twists and turns upward, seeming to defy an automobile to bend itself around the curves.

It is a different, a separate, a distinct setting from Liz's earlier homes. It is a place to begin again for the second time, and the need for a new beginning or second life is no unique experience for women today, Liz immediately points out. "One evidence of its prevalance is that there are women's centers all over the country offering courses with titles such as 'What Shall I Do with the Rest of My Life?' In Austin the day such a course was announced there were three times as many women signed up as could be enrolled. We're all realizing that we'll live to be 75.9 if we're lucky and stay off certain airlines. And what are we going to do with all those years?"

When we arrived, the fireplace at Grass Roots was glowing

with the first fire of the season, and the warmth reached out to fill the yellow-and-white room. It reflected on pieces of glass, photographs, sketches, and the memorabilia of a good, rich life in full motion. The windows at the end of the room revealed an unbroken view of the Austin, Texas, hills rising and falling into the distance with their load of autumn leaves bright under the morning sun.

But the warmest and brightest thing in the room was the ebullient Liz. She threw open the doors etched with designs of Texas grasses and pulled us, without hesitation, into the circle of her friendship.

She introduced us quickly to a visitor, a secretary, and a housekeeper. Then without ever breaking the train of her thought, she delved back into her years in Washington with Les at her side and the constant challenges of her job as press secretary at the White House. Then she spoke of the present. "I have everything now except one thing. I lost Les in 1972, and now there is no one person in the world to whom I am the most important being alive. My life is separate and apart from the thirty-five years in Washington, and in a sense it is a new beginning, a second life."

It was a wise friend who told her that her new life was in fact a second life, and not a continuation of her earlier life.

"I tried to stay in Washington after Les's death, but Washington was 'our' city and not 'mine,' so eventually I came back here. I'm rebuilding a life around one, not two. I couldn't have done it in Washington; there were too many ghosts."

Liz's thoughts jump back to the beginning of her second life, which was forced upon her with cruel suddenness by the heart attack Les suffered in Washington.

"He had put me on the plane that morning. He always took me to the airport and strangely that particular time he asked me several times the name of the group I was speaking to.

"I flew to Houston. Then, as was so often the case when I was off somewhere making a speech, he called to tell me what the political gossip in Washington was. Since a lot of my

Liz Carpenter is a journalist, co-chairperson of ERAmerica, founder of the National Women's Political Caucus, former executive assistant to President Lyndon Johnson and press secretary to Lady Bird Johnson. She is now building her second life after the death of her husband, Leslie Carpenter.

speech was topical humor I depended on him to keep me up with the gossip in Washington at that moment, and it always added a punch because whatever the big, riding political story is, people jell around it.

"Then he called me later in the day and told me two or three things I needed to know; I remember how full of excitement he sounded. Then I went in and made my speech.

"Later that night about twelve, after I'd gone to sleep, the phone rang and my son was suddenly saying that it was the hardest phone call he'd ever made. He said, 'Daddy's just dropped dead in Washington.' And so those were the words that changed my life.

"I was totally unprepared, although we had had some hints of problems. He had had some ill health, some hepatitis, and one thing and another.

"I doubt if the attack could have been avoided but he probably should have quit some tasks earlier—I mean he should have changed jobs before he did. And that's one of the things I think we have got to learn if we're to survive. We may need to move into a less-stressed area of work as we grow older. We've got to have two or three professions warmed up on the back burner, and I say this to commencement classes now because technology changes, and the world changes, and people have to change with it. What is a money-making profession at one time is not at another, and that affects our entire work experience, and possibly even the length of our lives if we are not adapted for change.

"No matter how much you enjoy your work, it just may not remain a viable field for your entire life, and this is hard for us all to understand."

Liz remembered the rush back to Washington where Les was dead at fifty-two as she said, "The champagne of life was flat. There was now no person on earth to whom I was *first.*"

She recalled Lady Bird's call two weeks later from Italy, where she was vacationing, and she remembered her urging to "walk away" from it all and spend a week or two in Florence.

For two weeks, Liz "walked away" from the thank-you notes and the hundreds of chores which cluster around death and was amazed at how distance could help her forget for awhile. "The dullness was still inside, but there was diversion from grief and you could almost pretend it hadn't happened while your strength returned and shock subsided."

Liz points out the need for such an escape from grief when beginning a second life. But she is realistic; she knows that not everyone can escape to Florence for days with a companion such as Lady Bird who had been her friend since the earliest days in Washington. But she feels that somewhere there is an escape for everyone, an escape for rest and the beginning of recovery. "You have to seek peace in a more detached setting," she observed. "Though it doesn't come at once."

"Racing" characterized the next period after her return to Washington. Always "racing," trying to escape memories of shared parties, shared evenings in a yard where Les had planted dogwood and azaleas, shared meals cooked with joy in anticipation of friends' arrival for dinner. There seemed to be a need to move, to hurry, to outrun the thoughts from the past.

Weekends were especially unbearable, and Liz found herself racing to accept speaking engagements or gatherings to fill up the lonely remembering time. She raced in the company of friends and alone. "Going out was not a problem," as she says, "People in Washington long ago stopped thinking the world came in twos, like Noah's ark. It was being at home that got to me. I had never been alone at home."

So there were too many things to remember on weekends. There were too many good memories playing about on the screen of her mind.

"One summer when our children were small we sat on the beach and had two weeks of the real joy of little children selling sea shells on the shore and of me cooking. I remember it rained for a whole week. What do you do with children four and two when it's raining on the beach? The grapes were in season, and I went out, bought a lot of grapes, got a lot of fruit jars, and we made grape jelly for four days in this cottage we'd rented. The smell of it was so glorious. We sat around and ate grape jelly because we couldn't resist it. The smell is a part of the whole memory. Grape jelly was our Christmas present that year, jars and jars for everyone.

"Then, there was one winter in Washington when it snowed us in. We lived at the end of a dead-end street and the whole town had thawed, but we didn't know it; the snow was still deep where we were. We made hot soup, built a snow man, and celebrated just being away from cares and enjoying the wonder of snow. Those are the kinds of things that come back as perfect times."

She recalls, "There was a period after our children were grown and gone when we had a Saturday adventure and each Saturday we'd reach out for a beautiful experience. It was a good balm. Sometimes we'd take a walk out on Roosevelt Island; there's a lovely channel house there in Georgetown. We'd have lunch out, and then go and shop and buy something we liked. Nearly all the pretty things in this house—a set of dessert dishes, a painting, a vase—are things we picked out together as a part of our Saturday adventure. Saturdays were slow and loving days, doing just as we liked and really being with each other."

Such memories continued to come back during grief after Les' death, so Liz raced on to escape their poignancy.

After two years, Liz found herself still unable to slow down. She finally realized it was the time to do something entirely, dramatically different. She realized that nothing was going to change as long as she stayed where she was in a house that was no longer, as she says, "my home" and a city which was not really "my city." It was from the world of her first life, and that life had ended.

Liz faced the hundreds of adjustments she would need to make if she left Washington. She considered the plans which must be made if she were to move to another city. She faced the objections and logical arguments of friends who pointed out that she almost had her lovely home paid for, and that the world of politics and political friends which had always been so important to her was centered in Washington. There were so many reasons to stay, but Liz realized in what she calls her "blind misery" that she could not live a complete second life in the haunting backyard of a first life.

To move was an agony of change; to remain was to hover in an agony of emptiness in a house which was no longer home. "I just didn't live there anymore," she said. But in order to move there must be another job and another house somewhere, but where?

Plans began to fall into shape as Lady Bird Johnson opened a door by offering Liz a job as consultant at the Lyndon B. Johnson Library in Austin. Offers for magazine articles began to come in. These were especially available since Liz was from the South and the then new president was from Georgia. It meant that she could speak with authority on the region the country was discovering through President Carter.

Liz now had a job and a city, the city where she had lots of relatives and old school friends from the University of Texas. She now only needed a home.

She knew the kind of house she wanted. The house must have a view of water, either a lake or the winding Colorado River, and it must have a view of the city. The hills around Austin offered a parapet with the possibility for both views. Her niece found the house, and it even went several steps beyond Liz's guidelines. It also had a separate guest house that would serve as a writing office for typewriter, files, and the accumulation of notes from thirty-five years in Washington. In addition to the required view of the water and the city, it offered a view of the Capitol Dome and the University of Texas Tower. It was right. It was "Grass Roots," and it only needed the grasses etched on the glass doors to prove its name. In a little more than three months it was to be called "home," the second home for the second life.

The second home was now a reality. The second life could now begin. But it did not begin by magic; it began by plan and careful design.

Liz took stock of herself, of her abilities, her likes and dislikes, and also those little things which would spell defeat to her second life it they were not recognized.

On the plus side she listed her writing ability which provided not only an activity and a job, but also constant contact with the outstanding people in the country. "I had held a variety of jobs—written a column called 'Southern Accents,' worked for the United Press, and had covered Congress for a group of papers in the South. When I started out, my 'office' had been a kind of dirty brown envelope that I carried around Capitol Hill with my copy in it. Later, of course, Les and I had offices in the National Press Building where we covered the White House and the Capitol. I felt at ease in the world of politics and work."

She was independent, she knew how to make arrangements and travel alone. She was not carrying the burdens of the widow who approached her after a speech with the question, "How do you go through airports all by yourself?"

She had the constant access to a podium and access to identity. She had the stimulation of living in both a man's and a woman's world which she quickly evaluated by saying, "That's the most interesting work, one that has both sexes." In fact, she adds, "I think a bit of the motive for women wanting to work is that they want to move into the interesting world outside, and the home alone just isn't that interesting."

She also had two successful children of whom she says with her famous grin, "I didn't have to worry about them, just love them."

Another confessed plus was her enthusiastic enjoyment of characters—zany, interesting people. She began to realize that there must be some compensation in the second life or it was indeed doomed, and this enjoyment of a variety of characters was perhaps a part of this compensation. She explained that Les had always enjoyed people who were more traditional.

She hunted for the adjective to describe what she meant and finally came up with "stylized, fitting one mold, and having the same ideas."

She said, "We had mostly entertained his type of friends in our home, and now I invite all types in for an evening." Growing philosophical Liz said, "I guess I am psychologically looking for ways to get even with death by showing it that I can realize some good things from it. One way I can do this is by doing something I would not have done if death had not intervened. I invite in some of those people who talk about everything and are simply more devil-may-care. I guess we are looking for ways to whip death at least a little. And besides, isn't it awful that couples think they both have to agree on a set of friends? So many couples settle on people they both like fairly well and miss out on the ones that really appeal to one or the other. So they just neutralize their guests—no reds, no greens, just a lot of grey."

Writing ability, contacts, independence, identity, children, and friends—these were the pluses for Liz as she entered her second life, but there were the minuses, too.

She spotted them immediately. "I just missed being needed. I am maternalistic by nature toward people, toward humanity, and I now felt rejected by fate."

She said, "I felt that I had missed my family long enough. Washington was 1,200 miles from my extended family, and I could in my second life come back and correct this minus. I could be near nieces and nephews and see my brothers and sister more often.

"But beyond my yearning to be needed by my family there was a yearning to contribute to something, some cause which was a part of myself. I found that in the ERA. I had been interested in the ERA earlier but suddenly I had the time to give to it. Also, I just didn't want to be left out of a movement that was affecting my sex. Why should I sit on the sidelines? I'm not a sidelines person, and I wanted to be in on the decisions that were being made.

"The largest number of families now have two breadwinners. Today's American family is not a man and a woman and two well-scrubbed children. That's less than 14 percent. The largest number of families have two moneymakers, and even beyond the economics there is just the fact that we women want to be all we can be in our span of time on this planet. We want to grow to be full human beings—totally whatever is in us, whatever our talents are.

"Further, I feel very strongly that we need ERA because we were left out of the Constitution purposely in 1778. I want the dignity of being in the constitution of my own country. We need the backup of the U.S. Constitution to establish that sex, as well as race, is not to be a point of discrimination.

"While the debate about the ERA has led to many positive changes, these do not reduce the need for the amendment. All of the laws could be easily changed, and new threats to equality of rights under the law could still be mounted under new guises if a guarantee is not enshrined in the Constitution.

"The new laws are not universal. Five of the eight community-property states have given wives co-management rights, but three have not. Only a few states have recognized the contribution of the homemaker as a factor to be considered in dividing property at divorce."

Liz is not only a believer in the cause, she is a highly verbal proponent and she hurries on, listing its advantages.

"Another important reason why the ERA is necessary is the leverage it gives for seeking the fundamental changes in domestic relations and property law, changes that will achieve the goal of marriage as a full partnership.

"I feel very strongly about the Equal Rights Amendment, and I did a lot of studying on how we got left out of the Constitution in the first place. It really is an angering point when you realize that if Abigail Adams had gone to Philadelphia instead of John, or with John, women would have been written into the Constitution.

"The founding fathers who met to write the Constitution of

the new country used English Common Law as their frame of reference and slaves, the mentally unfit, Indians, and women were all considered 'chattel' under English common law. You know, Abigail Adams wrote the one letter to John to 'remember the ladies,' and John just laughed at it.

"I went to the Library of Congress to see if there was any described draft of the document mentioning women. I'd written enough drafts of presidential speeches to know how much is left on the cutting-room floor.

"The nearest thing was a petition signed by 14,000 women in New England, asking that slave girls be educated to the same degree as slave boys.

"Slavery was the big issue between the Southerners and Yankees in the early writing. But the authors of the Constitution hadn't even received that petition because it was signed by women."

Liz Carpenter moved on from the Equal Rights Amendment to some of the other areas that affect women, and which are of particular interest to her now.

She looks at marriage with a glance back at her own good marriage and another glance into the future. "I see very good relationships between the young people I know, and it is a lot more realistic than the old kind of stereotyped couple idea where you keep your mouth shut and just go along and nod yes, and then you'll be treated lovingly in the bedroom. I think that people are expecting more from life than that and the old system is awfully passé.

"Now there's no question that women now don't put up with as much as they used to, and you have more divorces. I have a feeling that's going to settle down some and maybe, you know, who's to say that we were meant to live forever with one man? I happen to have hoped that life would be that way for me. It seems ideal, but I'm not sure that it's written in the laws anywhere that that's the way life's going to work out best.

"Patterns for women have changed so much. The 'Sweetheart of Sigma Chi' is dead! Also, wealthy widows just are not remarrying. They have spent their lives ministering to a man, and they don't want to spend the rest of their time selecting the right necktie.

"It's interesting that when Jean Stapleton was trying to figure out how to characterize Edith Bunker in 'All In The Family,' she decided on the running metaphor. She felt the constant running from the kitchen to the front door expressed first that the series was set in New York which is a city under the pressure of motion. And second, it expressed that she was constantly serving at Archie's beck and call. So lots of people have been running, and lots of other people are changing their running patterns.

"But I do think that couples who live together with no marriage vows lose something in that there does not seem to be enough commitment. If you believe in each other you ought to have more faith than that, and I couldn't live without vows. But I must say there are an awful lot of young people I've looked at and known they're wrong for each other, and I've been so glad when they didn't tie themselves into something that was hard to back out of. And I guess we all have to adjust our old standards. The pill has made different life-styles possible."

Memory of her first life with Les reaches into her second life as she says, "Sex? Of course I miss sex. Any normal, healthy woman will." But when a friend advised an affair, Liz said, "If you grew up in the Bible Belt, this is no solution."

A second life requires energy, and Liz says that she sometimes uses more energy than she really has. "My best hours are in the morning, and I'm up early and I'm Captain Bligh. On with the shoes! I'm in charge! I'm wondering why everyone is sleeping. I like to get a lot accomplished. I like action and movement; my father was like this. What I like is a fast, productive day, and good conversation and entertainment in the evening."

Liz had opened the door to her childhood with the mention of her father, and we reached in to discover the kind of childhood which prepared her for change and new experiences.

"I grew up in a house that had people coming and going. While it might be confusing to some people, it just seemed the most normal thing in the world for it not to be just an in-house kind of family. It gave me a lot of elasticity in my life.

"When I went to the University of Texas the matriculation fee was $12.50. My mother took a house in Austin, and we just opened it to all the cousins. There was an openness of spirit there that just caught on.

"Besides the elasticity I gained, I also acquired very early a tremendous sense of history and a feel for politics.

"I had a mother who quoted from the English poets as she washed the dishes and swept up after five children and our household. I grew up in Salado in the oldest house in Texas continuously inhabited by the same family, and I was always conscious of having a strong strain of leadership in my ancestors. They were people who had been achievers; one had written the Texas Declaration of Independence, another had brought 600 colonists to the then-unsettled land. I had a relative who died at the Alamo, and maybe from these events I felt a compulsion to be somebody, to do something with my energy.

"One room in our house marked me for life. It was a cool parlor where there were books which had been brought from Tennessee and Virginia. It had all the good smells of leathery old books.

"There were photographs around the house of eight beautiful women, strong women who were family members. One had been the first Democratic National Committeewoman.

"My great grandmother's written words are preserved there. She had penned them to free her thirty slaves with a formal declaration, 'Due to the failure of the Confederate cause . . .' So, from this influence we all grew up with a strong sense of our heritage. In those days we didn't use the words of middle class or upper class, but we felt somehow that we were members of the aristocracy. So I think I was very privileged to have this kind of assurance as a child. I was Mary Elizabeth Sutherland in those days," Liz added.

We asked if she felt any sense of loss of identity by growing up with one name and then losing that name almost totally as she moved into adult life as Liz Carpenter.

She answered, "Yes, I think that there is no question that a lot of what shaped me was Sutherland, and a lot that shaped me was Robertson, and I don't have that identity in my name. I probably wouldn't turn back the clock, but I think a woman probably feels the loss more in widowhood when her husband is no longer with her. In my case, the Carpenter part of my life is no longer a daily thing and yet that is my name. Maybe the Latins have the right idea in hyphenating and retaining their complete names."

The statement about her name reflected something we had noticed earlier about Liz. She looked back to things that could have been different and maybe even should have been different, but she carried little regret or disappointment into her second life. Maybe that is one of the explanations for the bounce in her emotional step.

She does have some regret as she says, "I'm sorry I wasn't smarter. If I could go back and pick up a few things, I would have gone to Smith or Radcliffe for a year when I was much younger. I'd have worked a little harder and made Phi Beta Kappa and Mortar Board. That's about it." Then, with the flash of a sudden smile, she said, "I'm disappointed that I can't sing. I only wish I sang. I think singing would be the greatest way to express your moods and heart."

We asked about the singing and found a deep stream of feeling running back to the time when the Sutherlands all sang around a piano. "Music was important, but not the great operas, just singing. I had lots of aunts who sang in the choir in the Methodist church, but when we were together it wasn't just religious songs we sang. At gatherings we sang and we talked politics. Somebody said that Texas didn't have horse racing, and we didn't have legalized liquor, so we took all our vices out in politics. There's a whole world of politics that's part of the conversation in the South and it's the reason we send a lot of people to Congress who make a life's work out of it."

"The gift of oratory, the gift of story-telling is likely to spring up in a society of this kind. I believe you find it is richest in more rural parts of the country. But there was certainly good conversation at our home. You didn't talk chit chat and talk about money was crass. And so we were much more likely to be talking about what's happening in the Capital or life outside of ourselves."

We asked Liz's opinion of the saying that Southern children grow up with politics and literature while Eastern children grow up with art and music. We wondered if that seemed accurate to her.

"Well, art had been something that had come to Texas late, I think, because we were a frontier state and art probably comes late to any frontier. First, people with money would run off and buy what they'd heard was good, and they pretty soon discovered that what was around them was pretty good. I think we've just learned to live comfortably with good art.

"Art and music are a beautiful source of strength in life at any stage, and everybody is searching for something to hang onto. We search for it at different times in our lives.

"Men around fifty years old sometimes go through an aging process and come out stomach-ulcered and crotchety, and women at that same age have just reared their children and are ready to move onto something more interesting. So women especially are searching, and art is frequently a part of the treasure."

Liz moved easily from women's searches into her own life pattern of work and children. "My life did not follow the pattern of staying at home and then opening up, since I have always worked, and since my husband and I were in the same profession, we were both available as parents. If a child had the whooping cough Les or I, depending on who could leave the job more easily at that moment, went home. Besides, I liked working at home; I didn't have to put on a tight girdle and be uncomfortable while I worked.

"I learned how to tune everything out. My kids would tell me they had talked to me and I didn't even know it because I was concentrating so hard. They would say, 'Are you tuned in?' "

We wondered if Liz felt that she could have stayed at home without any outside work for twenty years of child rearing. Could she have been content?

"I think I could have; I wonder what I would have been like. Even my house would have been over-cleaned and over-decorated. I would have to use my energy up some way. I would have over-cooked and over-scrubbed. I would have over-done everything. I would have been into clubs that probably were not very meaningful, and I wouldn't have been earning any money to contribute to the family till. I have never really known how to do things slowly and to relax, and in some ways that has been a handicap. There were a few times in my marriage when I wondered what it would be like just to be a pampered wife.

"Also there were a few times when I wondered what it would be like if Les and I did not have the conversation about politics and the office, when it would be just candle light, one to one, man and woman in conversation. We had a very loving marriage, but there were a few times I wondered that. There was only once when I really went anywhere where we weren't both involved. That was when Les was on a Navy Board and I went along: I thought, *Gosh, I don't have to do anything at this. I don't have to make a speech; I don't have to say anything; he's the one. I just have to look pretty at dinner.* I think I bathed with all the great soaps they had in the room, and I really liked it. Perhaps there should have been more times like that. It's what you hope will be later on and what we were beginning to get into with both children graduating from college.

"But, really, life is a collection of moments, of good moments and lousy moments, but you learn to reach for those fine moments. The times I enjoyed best were good conversation, good friends, relaxation, where people were really talking about things outside of themselves, not chatting about the mundane. I don't want to hear about the children and the grandchildren, unless it's pertinent. When I'm laughing spontaneously, I am lifted. I like to laugh spontaneously. I like to be around my funny friends. Looking back I realize that somebody once said wisely that life is what's happening to you while you're planning ahead. It makes me realize that I should have cherished all the good things more along the way. You can find a thrill in a moment from a podium when you know you're speaking to the hearts of people out there and you can sense it. That's a sense of power, too. Somebody comes up to you and says you wrote a letter that helped them get a job; that's a good feeling.

"We had a lot of personal moments of intimacy that meant a lot. But life really isn't just made up of perfect moments. It's made up of some tough times and sometimes in the toughest times you grow the most. I think when you're feeling used up is the best time. When I die I want to be all used up. I don't want there to be anything left. And when you are having to think harder or having to laugh more or when you are living the ultimate, that's the best. It's all very good to talk about quiet relaxation, and all that kind of stuff, but I doubt if you really are growing with that. I think the time you grow is when you're tugging on a lot of things in you to fulfil that moment. I feel like I've been a happy woman, and yet I cannot say that life is completely happy now, because there are always missing gaps; you're missing something, but you should be just happy that it is as good as it is.

"It's the same way with marriage, and I think young people should realize that it too is not made up just of perfect moments. The seventh year is lousy. You know, marriage is like wine; there are good years and bad years, and you're crazy to walk away from something simply because it's gone sour or vinegary at that time. The times of feeling the real pressures and stress for me were when I had been working as a reporter, and we were swept up in Washington, and suddenly I had these two small children and it dawned on me, they do cry. Babies do cry. You do have to have somebody responsible to take care of them; it's just crazy to think that you can be super-woman and carry everything. But in our case, we got good help and that saved me.

"I think you have to be willing to pay for good help when you work, and you should not make all your decisions on the basis of mathematics and money.

"Les was as interested in having good help as anybody, and we never sat down and did the figuring of whether it really would be cheaper if I would stay home and be a housekeeper. Now that's where I think the young woman today really makes an error. It shouldn't be a matter of her money that's paying that helper; it should be *their* money. It's whether they want to live life to the fullest. And if life to the fullest depends upon her working somewhere outside the home, then why count nickels and dimes? The alternative is to spend your life doing something you don't like at all well.

"But the kind of help you need may not be the stereotyped idea of help. You want somebody who helps you live the kind of life you want to live. Removing cobwebs in the corner is not the most important thing when your kids are a certain age. They need a loving person, or maybe they need someone who drives. Maybe you all need someone who can do the shopping and pick up clothes at the cleaners. I now have somebody who can pick up parcels, or sew on buttons, and mail my column. She's a lousy cook, but who can do everything?"

Liz feels strongly that decisions about the kind of help you need or whether you need help at all are important decisions, like the hundreds of other choices which determine the quality of your life. First life or second life involves decision-making, and Liz feels that she decides quickly.

She sums it all up, "Maybe some people would say that I'm impulsive, that I live impulsively, that I just don't take a long time making decisions, but I have regretted very few that I have made. I am not an indecisive person who worries and nurses something to death. I want to reach a conclusion. Les was the love of my life, but he is gone, and I have a lot of good memories of the past, but I also have a heck of a lot of good plans for the future.

"There's so much to be done, and I want to be a good, moving part of it. As I said, I want to use up everything that's in me and be everything for which I have any potential. That's the most important decision of all, just to go on being challenged and interested constantly."

Ida Luttrell is a wife and the mother of four children. She is not employed outside her home, although she has a degree in bacteriology and has worked for Texas Children's Hospital. She is completely content to be home-centered in a period when many women are looking for satisfaction outside the home environment.

4. Ida Luttrell

Fulfillment in Her
Home and Family

"And then he was born. That was the most wonderful thing that had ever happened to me in my life. It was just delightful to have a baby at home by himself. Because, you see, by the time he was born the other children were in school all day, and I didn't have the hassle of all these others demanding my attention."

Shortly after we arrived at Ida Luttrell's home we asked if she had ever experienced a perfect moment in her life. She replied, "Yes, I can say that I have had a perfect moment in my life; in fact, I had one just recently in this very room." Ida Luttrell gazed off into space for a moment before she went on. "We weren't doing anything in particular. It was just that all the children were here and we were together. As I remember, Anne was playing the piano."

It is no accident that Ida's perfect moment occurred in the midst of home and children, for to Ida home and children are the richest sources of joy and color in the texture of life. But there are so many other threads of both dark and light intensities in the pattern. There is no monotone here; life on Beauregard Street in an upper-middle-class home is not always smooth or without tension. It is far from perfect, but as Ida says without hesitation, "Yes, I am very content."

Why is Ida content in a society where discontent among non-career women is frequently the style as well as the fact? Is it because she is without ambition? Brainwashed? Unimaginative? We learned it was none of these in an interview which proved to be like a Sunday afternoon on a deep couch by a glowing fireplace—with the stimulation of an occasional snowball from the outside world thrown powerfully into our faces.

Perhaps Ida's ability to be content in her life situation began in her childhood which, as she says, was not just everybody's average childhood.

She said, "I grew up in South Texas which is predominately Mexican-American. I lived out on a ranch and had four sisters and one brother. My family was like two families because there was an age gap in between the three youngest children and the three oldest children. So I felt like my oldest sister was more like a second mother to me, and I felt close to my two younger sisters. We lived out in the country in a cold house. People don't think of South Texas as cold, but that house was hard to heat—and it was very cold in the winter.

"I would say my family was basically happy; my parents were older than most parents. My dad was almost fifty when I was born, a situation I don't recommend because he was too fearful for us children. I think younger parents aren't afraid of ordinary things so much. Mother was just the opposite; she never particularly worried although she was thirty-seven or thirty-eight when I was born. She has always been a guiding light for me because she has overcome so many obstacles.

"My daddy just adored us. The family was his life. But he was a worrier which made him strict with us."

Ida discussed her early schooling by saying, "I went to school and rode the school bus and had some very good teachers. Of course, some very poor teachers, too. I would say one of the people who influenced my life, beyond my parents, was probably my first-grade teacher who was a very kind person. I really felt she gave me some attention. Mother was a very busy person and was not able to give each of us as much attention as she would have liked. Also, she's not the type of person who's going to smother a child. She loved us very much, and I felt this love when I was growing up."

Ida recalls that she was a good student and that this was

what brought her recognition in her family. She couldn't be a part of activities such as band because staying after school to practice would have meant that someone had to drive seven miles into town to pick her up. So, she says, "We just didn't participate."

She remembers the bus rides and she recalls a friend who rode with her. "We had so much fun, and she'd come out and spend the night with me, and that's what our social life consisted of."

There just wasn't a lot for a child to do in Hebbronville but go to the movies and this was not a possibility for Ida because her daddy thought that was a "bunch of nonsense." There was very little cultural exposure, but there was a library. She liked to read, so she did have this advantage.

The high school was mostly Mexican-American, and at that time Anglos and Mexican Americans did not mix socially. "So," as Ida says, "aside from the junior-senior proms and a few parties, I had a very dull social life in high school. So, I can't tell you I had a typical, average, middle-class American childhood growing up, because I didn't."

There was never any question, though, about whether the children would go to college. "My parents, particularly my dad, because he had a very limited education, wanted so much for us to go. My dad said that education is something that no one can take away from you. And mother was in favor of it, too. Mother had gone to college one year, but daddy had not gone beyond the fourth grade and he could see how it had held him back all of his life. Like kids from the beginning of time, I couldn't wait to go to college! I couldn't wait to kiss Hebbronville goodbye."

Ida saw some of her own emotions repeated, although the circumstances were vastly different with her own son. She told us, "When our eldest son, Bob, left for college this fall, it brought back memories of my leaving home for the first time. One thing I remember about my starting to college was that my brother had sent me this enormous suitcase for a graduation gift. I was so proud of that, but since I was going to ride the bus, I needed boxes to pack the rest of my things. Mother said, 'I've got just the boxes for you.' She went to the dairy barn and returned with two large boxes milking machines had been packed in. On the outside of the boxes were pictures of milking machines. I nearly died. 'When I get to college they are going to know I'm from the country. I don't need to advertise it,' I told her. But I did take those boxes and one of my best friends, Patty Lunz, who was going to major in pharmacy, and I boarded that bus and left for college. We were beside ourselves with joy, but I was so green and raw."

She remembers her years at the university, living in a co-op in a converted Victorian mansion. Most of the girls living there were from farm families or they were preachers' daughters and Ida recalls, "I loved it! I loved it!"

She wanted to be a library science major but she found that it took five years; however, she worked in the library. At the age of eighteen it appeared that the people working there were little, fusty whispering souls tiptoeing around, so she decided "Oh ye gads, I don't want to do this." But she adds, "But I loved the books, and at this moment in my life, I would like to go back and get a degree in library science. Work in a library still appeals to me, but at eighteen that was just too dull and too tame."

Ida liked science and she had an excellent science teacher in high school, but she was afraid that she couldn't pass the college courses. "I just didn't have enough confidence in myself to take some of the math and science courses." Her new roommate was a bacteriology major. She said, 'Well, if you like science you will love this.' She said, 'You're doing great in biology. Why don't you take freshman chemistry? If you pass freshman chemistry you can pass all the chemistry.' "

Chemistry was what Ida was afraid of and she had to take twenty hours for the degree. She dared to take freshman chemistry and made a B in it; from then on she majored in bacteriology and loved it.

Her father's heart attack, her mother's illness from trying to care for him and run a dairy, and the threat of her younger sister having to drop out of high school to help with the dairy caused Ida to leave college during her junior year. As the situation improved, she was back at the university.

She recalls her decision to work at Texas Children's Hospital after she finished her degree. "I had always loved babies and little children. I knew that the children would be sick, but I didn't realize that there would be depressing parts of the work, but even so I think that job gave me more confidence in myself than anything else. I just didn't have a lot of confidence until I got that job. I worked hard and they made me feel like they couldn't do without me. I felt very needed."

Ida found these years particularly pleasant. She lived with five girls and she felt so free; their time was their own except for working hours. There were no classroom assignments to prepare for tomorrow, and on the weekend there were no responsibilities except to get in the car and head for the beach. She stopped to say, "I would recommend to young people that they not get married until they're out of college for awhile. For me this was a unique time for supporting myself. I was on my own, and it was just a wonderful time of independence."

There was a difference then in the attitude toward marriage. "This was back in the days when if you didn't get married you were an 'old maid,' and nobody wanted to be an old maid." Ida says with fervor, "Thank goodness, women today don't have to worry about that stigma."

Ida worked for eight years and then she met Bill Luttrell. The day he asked her to marry him still stands out in Ida's mind as one of the happiest and most exciting days of her life.

They became engaged in December and were married in January in a very quiet ceremony because Bill is a very quiet person and did not want a lot of fanfare.

She continued to work after the wedding, and they didn't plan to have any children for several years. Things worked out differently, though, and in November—only ten-and-a-half months later—their first child was born. Ida says, "I had always loved babies and now I had one of my very own. The only thing I regretted was that I had to leave him with a maid and go back to work. I wanted so much to stay with him and care for him myself. Nora, the black woman who took care of him, was an excellent substitute mother. But after two years, she became ill and had to quit working so I put Bob in a day nursery."

She has thought much of those days and has listened to what others say about leaving children. "Several years after this I took a course in human growth and development taught by Dr. Alma Malone at Houston Baptist University. It was interesting to hear her say it had been shown that the effect of separation of mother from child among working mothers is harder on the mother. I believe that is true. It was for me."

Ida spoke poetically of the arrival of her next child three years later. "On a golden day in October, Anne was born. My joy was complete and I thought my family was, too. A boy and a girl, every family's dream. One year after Anne was born we were financially able for me to quit work and stay home with the children. As much as I loved my job and the wonderful people I had met during the eight years I worked there, I was happy to leave and be at home with Bob and Anne.

"I was in for a big surprise. Staying home and taking care of two small children and a home, after leaving it to a maid while I went to work every day, took some adjustment. As much as I wanted to stay home and as much as I loved my children, I was lonely and desperate for adult companionship. Bill came to my rescue by insisting that I get a maid to help me so I could get out once or twice a week. Then a lovely neighbor moved next door to me. We spent a lot of time together, with the children under foot, and it was wonderful. It saved my sanity. It was so marvelous to have someone I could share with. I felt so lucky to have someone with similar interests, someone I could carry on an adult conversation with."

Ida was making her adjustment but when Anne was eighteen months old, along came Billy. She remembers it as hectic at times. "When I had the three little ones it really was kind of manic. People manage with more, but I don't know how they do it. I'll tell you how I managed with three. I gave up any idea of being the world's greatest housekeeper. The diapers stayed in the dryer until I got around to folding them for use; that's the the way I handled it. Bill has never complained about my housekeeping, bless his soul. Now that I have more time, while I don't get great pleasure from doing housework, I do enjoy having the house straight and clean. I enjoyed it then, too, but I knew it was impossible, so I just didn't let it bother me too much."

Ida's memories of Billy's birth are mixed with pictures of her mother coming to help her. "Billy was born early on a Sunday morning, a beautiful day, and mother had come to Houston with a friend, and was there when I brought him home. I enjoyed having her with me, and I think it was a treat for her, too, because she had never been able to be with any of the grandchildren when they were born. It's strange that all my life I worried about mother, and I think it was because she was my source of security. I felt very close to mother. You know, she was my lifeline.

"I remember when she taught school when I was small, one time she had a bad cold and I was afraid she would get pneumonia. She had a playground duty and I could see her outside my classroom window. It was cold and drizzling and I was so afraid she would get wet. I came home that afternoon and she was lying on the bed, which was very unusual for her. I just knew she was going to die. Well, she's eighty-two years old and still will probably outlive me. Things come up, and I think, 'My gosh, stop worrying about your mother! If anybody is going to make it, she is.' "

The birth of the new baby was followed by what Ida says is the saddest thing that has ever happened to her. "When Billy was six months old, Carrie Lee, my youngest sister, died. During the time she was sick, I wanted so much to help her and be with her, but I had three small children to take care of at home. She was a very vivacious person and her death left a great, jagged, empty hole in our family."

The death of her sister caused her to look at life differently. One change was that it brought her back into the church because she felt a great need for God after the loss. She recalls, "You go through something like that and you're just not capable, or I wasn't, of handling it myself. I wonder how people who profess not to have a faith manage tragedies.

"It is strange that when Billy was small he was a very solemn child and never smiled much. Some say a child reflects your attitude and I thought, *well, I probably never smiled much during those months because it was the time of her illness and death. But anyway — isn't this ridiculous? Crying over something that happened so long ago.*"

There was a lengthy pause before Ida could go on, but then with characteristic optimism she put the sadness behind her as she went back to thoughts of her child.

"But Billy turned into such a happy child. Parents worry too much about things that correct themselves, and each child is so different and special in his own way. Bob is thoughtful with a tremendous sense of humor. Anne is generous and has a great inner strength, and Richard is a loving child. He has a lot of empathy with people."

Ida admits being a person who is always looking around the next bend in the road. So when her third child went to preschool three mornings a week, she decided to go back to the university and prepare herself to teach if it should ever be necessary for her to work.

She decided to teach rather than return to the hospital because she felt it would be more compatible with the children's schedule. "I just enjoyed college thoroughly, and I had some development courses that taught me a lot. I wish I had had that before I had my first child. It's too bad we aren't trained seriously for motherhood—we only train to teach someone else's child."

In the fall of 1970 she enrolled again. That year Billy was in kindergarten, and Ida had more time and could see her teaching certificate on the horizon. She was scheduled to have a hysterectomy in January, but when she went to the doctor in November for a checkup she discovered she was pregnant!

"What a surprise! I had to rearrange my plans and my thinking. And then Richard was born. That was the most wonderful thing that could have happened. It was just delightful to have a baby at home by himself because by the time he was born the other children were in school all day and I didn't have the hassle of so many demanding my attention."

We asked why the birth of this fourth baby was such an especially happy event, and we asked why she felt it was so satisfying.

She felt it is partially because his birth made her appreciate the gift of being able to bear children. "You see, it was kind of like a miracle that he was born, because of the circumstances surrounding my physical condition. It was a situation where it was almost impossible for me to conceive a child, and the chances for carrying him to full term were not good. Each one of my children is very special to me, but there was nothing unusual about the other births. Having a small baby in the family drew us together as a family. I tell Bill that Richard was meant to be, that he was given to us for a special purpose. I don't know what it is, maybe just to make Bill and me happy. It made me realize that each of our children, each person in the world, in fact, is meant to be. We are all here for a reason."

We asked if she had any misgivings about dropping out of college, but she confessed that college had not been a burning desire with her, and she much preferred taking care of a baby to continuing her work. She also felt that she could go back to college later if she wanted to.

In view of her interrupted education, Ida has considered what she would do if she should ever find it necessary to work to support her family.

"The smart thing for me to do would be to go out to Bill's office and learn his business, but that is not my thing. I'm like my daddy—I would be just swallowed up in five minutes if I had to fight the business world. I just don't have whatever it takes. I'm like a marshmallow, I guess, when it comes to dealing with people. Bill is primarily in insurance now and there's a plan where his firm gives the wife six months to learn and take over his accounts. He told me I could do that with no problem, and maybe if I had to that would be the best thing for me to do.

"I would rather be a librarian, though. That does not pay well at all, but I could be a school librarian and that would pay more than a county librarian. I noticed in the library the other day a list of county jobs available. The one for the janitor was $800 a month and the one for the librarian was $500 a month. Isn't that ridiculous? And I think it still takes a master's degree to be a librarian."

The thought of work was a practical view, but Ida also has a dream. In her daydreams she sees herself getting her first book published. She says this is her fantasy right now.

It is actually more than a fantasy though, since she has already had several articles on glass published, and she has been working on children's stories for sometime.

Her fantasy is no dream of glory—it is more a dream of a quiet happiness. In her mind's eye she is not walking into an autograph party and receiving applause. Instead, she is getting an acceptance in the mail instead of a rejection. She is holding the published book in her hand. She says, "I don't care a thing about any kind of fame, so why do I want the book? I don't know, I just want it. I'd just like to have a book that I wrote to hold in my hand."

Her other dreams are primarily dreams of her children. She dreams of them all growing up to be successful, but to her, "successful" doesn't mean that they all have to be professionals, just that they lead lives that make them happy.

She and her husband are both careful not to impress their daughter with the idea that she has to be married in order to be successful in life, and they are pleased that she appears to be very much her own person. Ida feels that she is very bright and can do anything she wishes in life. At the moment she is thinking of training as a certified public accountant, and both parents are pleased with this possibility.

Ida says that she would also like to see her daughter have a family. She hopes that she would be able to stay home with her children, but feels in this day it almost takes two incomes to support a family.

Ida thinks of her own temperament and her daughter's. "It just depends on how she feels about staying home with children. Now in my case, I wanted to be home. But I see many people who love children and want to have a family, but they just can't stand to stay home. They have to go out and work for the sake of their sanity. A mother working is much better than a crazy mother."

Earlier Ida had commented on the satisfaction of working for a few years after college and enjoying the independence before marriage. She came back to the idea as she thought of her own children.

"I think that a carefree period of life would be wonderful for any boy or girl, maybe more so for a boy. I think kids are restless when they are just out of college. They think they want to marry and a lot of people do and it works out fine, but I think it is better to experience the single life for awhile. It is fun, but not always as glamorous as it looks. I'm not saying that fun and adventure end with marriage, but it is a kind of independence and freedom from responsibility during that single period that you will probably never have again."

Since so much of Ida's life is centered around her marriage we asked her to share some of her convictions about marriage in an era of turbulence concerning marriage and divorce.

She thinks the secret of a durable marriage is not so much treating your spouse as you would like to be treated, as it is treating him as you treat your friends. "That's sometimes hard to do. I'm sometimes brought up short hearing myself say something to my husband that I wouldn't say to a friend, and I can't understand why we would say something sharp to someone we love that we wouldn't say to a friend."

We asked if she considered it a desirable goal to have an exciting marriage. She surprised us by saying, "What do you mean by an 'exciting marriage'? I hate to ask that because it sounds like mine must be dull. It's not really—we have an interesting life together."

In spite of her question, we felt the excitement in her voice as she told us, "It is exciting just to see Bill happy and laughing. In fact, the other night we went out and he just came walking across the lawn, he wasn't even dressed up, and I thought, *Well, gosh, he sure looks nice.* In fact, the highlight of my day is when he comes in that door from work."

Through the years since the time the children were small Bill and Ida have added a pleasant and very real event to each week. On Sunday afternoon they go for an excursion to see something. It may be a neighboring town, an old building, a museum, a park, or a picnic site, but regardless of where it is, they look forward to it as a big part of the week. "We've seen a lot of things over the years," Ida says, "and it has been such a good chance to be together as a family."

"Stable" is the word Ida thinks of in relation to this life together. The thought of separate vacations does not offend her, but she is quick to say she would prefer to vacation with Bill.

She hopes that her four children will follow traditional roles in marriage, but she is pretty sure of what her response would be if they did not. "I would try to talk to them, and if I had no success I would feel I had done all I could do. Once they get to be eighteeen years old, if they haven't caught on to what you want them to do, it's almost too late, really. You can do so much and, of course, there's a lot of pressure from the outside world that you have no control over."

Ida sees herself as a person who has common sense and is practical. She feels that she is shy, but she is working to overcome that. We could almost hear her stamping a mental foot as she said, "I'm going to try to improve that."

She feels little anger, and what she does experience is mostly toward people who crowd her on the freeways or do small, irritating things. Even speaking of these she is quick to say, "But I'm sure I irritate a lot of people, too."

She says that she likes most people, and she had recently spoken to her daughter about enjoying friends. She said, "Anne, I look at it this way, none of my friends are perfect, and I'm not either. If they have enough good qualities to outbalance the bad ones, I would just overlook any little things."

She doesn't recall that anyone has every done her a great injustice, and her warmest feelings come from remembering people, friendships, and family.

"Whenever my family comes here for Thanksgiving that just gives me the most wonderful feeling. Last spring when everything was getting very hectic with school winding up and Bob graduating, I would think, *Oh, Alice is moving close by in Richmond!* That really cheered me!"

The outlines of Ida's daily joys are clear, but she feels that she hasn't always had clear ideas of what she wanted to be or do. As a child she had no clear vision of herself in the future. She says, "I don't know what my desires were particularly. I knew I wanted to get a job and support myself. I just never looked beyond to an overall picture of how I would like to spend my life, and I still don't to this day."

Since Ida had commented on her openness to the future we tried to think of one of the heaviest jobs around to ask her how she would respond to being thrust into it. We asked what she would do if she discovered that Bill had just been elected president and she would become the First Lady in January.

She responded with a laugh, but she was far from overwhelmed at the thought. "I'd call Lady Bird Johnson. No, I don't know what I'd do." But immediately she was making practical suggestions. "I assume there are lots of people to tell you what to do about protocol and all. It wouldn't phase me to shake hands with Jimmy Carter or Gerald Ford or whomever. I think I would approach the job of First Lady as something that I wouldn't necessarily want to do, but that I pretty much had to do and would do the best I could."

It occurred to us that in that statement there might be a part of Ida's obvious contentment. Perhaps she approached everything practically with a resolve to "do the best I could." But certainly there was much more here; there was the constant enjoyment of Bill's coming home each evening, of Anne's playing the piano, and of the little activities of the children. There was the lack of anger and the inability to recall anyone who had every done her an injustice. There was the often expressed appreciation for other people, but perhaps even more important were the dreams—the dream for the children and the dream of the book to be published.

All of these elements were present in Ida's contentment at home, a home which she cares for, but in which she is by no means a prisoner.

Which elements are the most important we couldn't tell, but whichever they were, it was apparant that Ida meant it when she said, "Yes, I am very content with my life. Yes, I am fulfilled in the things I am doing here in my home." It was good to bask in her contentment.

5. Jane Wyatt

Television and Movie Actress with Strength

"I realized that I might as well settle down and enjoy life and not be desperate to get on with my career. So at that moment I changed my attitude. I realized that I had done something already, and I had gotten somewhere — and then I just enjoyed my life as it developed from there on."

To thousands of people Jane Wyatt will always be Margaret Anderson of television's "Father Knows Best." To an entire nation of viewers she literally became that person, and in reality she retains all of Margaret's charms. Yet, there are more dimensions to Jane than were ever captured in all the miles of film shot in the ideal Anderson home.

Jane is just as neat and perfectly turned-out as Margaret was on her most appealing episode. She also has just as much crinkley-eyed humor as any of us remember her using in dealing with her three television children and her storybook husband, Robert Young.

It is perhaps Jane's depth of personal wisdom, stamina, and determination which the 207 episodes of "Father Knows Best" did not quite reveal. There is also a current of unshakeable faith which we may not have sensed in the convincing personality which made Margaret Anderson so real to us. Any of these characteristics which were lost on the screen were certainly apparent as soon as we said hello to Jane, and she began to tell us of her life, tracing some of the strands which had enabled her to combine family and career, home and theater. She recalled frustrations in the early days, but she was quick to relate circumstances which made the mix of family and work easier to handle than it would have been if money worries or family opposition had been present.

Jane was born with the proverbial silver spoon in her mouth and blue blood coursing in her veins. She was dropped from the Social Register when she went into the theater, but this event seems of little significance to her when it is compared with her early and continuing desire to act.

She says that everybody thought her family would be violently opposed to her going on the stage, but the fact that family ties were deep with the theater created a different point of view. Her mother was a drama critic in New York for thirty-five years, reviewing for *Catholic World, Commonweal, Liturgical Arts,* and the *Dublin Review.* So the world of theater was indeed a part of daily life for Jane, so much in fact that she says, "I can't remember a day when I didn't want to act."

She grew up in New York City and later attended Barnard College. After two years she spent the summer in the Theater Apprentice School of the Berkshire Playhouse in Stockbridge, Massachusetts, and made the decision to gain some acting experience on the stage. She says, "So then I didn't get back for the last two years at Barnard. That may have been a mistake, but I didn't anyway. I went and walked up and down Broadway, and got my first part and my next part and my third part, and it just started off. That's how it started for me."

With a courage and determination which seem surprising in the warm, soft personality which Jane projects, she tells of fighting her way into casting offices in hopes of trying out for parts. She recalls the schedule vividly.

"Every morning at 10 I used to get all dressed up. I'd walk up and down Broadway and go up the stairs and down the stairs and in the elevator, and I'd give this long song and dance to the producers. You waited outside in those days. I don't know what they do now, but then you just bulldozed your way in. You knew someone was casting and when they asked you what you'd done, you made up a long story about the parts you'd played in school and college, and they all knew you

Jane Wyatt is known to a generation of television viewers as Margaret Anderson of "Father Knows Best," but in addition to this role she is known as the dramatic lead in many outstanding movies and plays. She is also a woman who has balanced home and career, theater and family, and come out with a deeply satisying life.

were stretching things. I looked about ten years old—round, fat face, and plump, and obviously too young to have all that experience."

She remembers those days as exciting. It's worthy of note to her that she was able to achieve most when she went alone and didn't surround herself with a group of other young, aspiring actors. Jane's independence is apparent as she looks back and recalls how much easier it was for her to deal with secretaries, producers, and closed doors when she was alone and making her own decisions.

Her move from Broadway to Hollywood followed a pattern which was common at that time. She says that you did parts in New York. Then "if you made a little splash on Broadway you were asked to go to Hollywood. Then you always said, 'Oh, no, no.' This was the thing to say; we always said we wanted to stay in New York and get more experience. So I stayed for awhile, and I was offered a lot of things but I had a bad year. So when they asked me again to go to Hollywood, I arranged to go just for the summer months. This was foolish because once you got out there, if the movie was not ready to start, you had to wait around for three months, and then when you eventually came back, the Broadway plays were already cast and you had missed out. So, after that first experience I just drifted to Hollywood little by little and stayed longer and longer."

The highly successful "Lost Horizons" with Ronald Colman was her second movie. It was followed by roles with co-stars Gregory Peck ("Gentleman's Agreement"), Cary Grant ("None But The Lonely Heart"), and Gary Cooper ("Task Force").

But even with this impressive list of successes it is probably her episodes of "Father Knows Best" which planted her most firmly in the American memory. The show won for her three Emmys, and it is still appearing in reruns, although the last segment was filmed in 1960.

As her career was flourishing, Jane Wyatt married Edgar

Bethune Ward, and she speaks of her marriage by saying, "We've been eternally happy, but he's not at all interested in the theater." They met on the train going to a party at the Hyde Park home of Franklin and Eleanor Roosevelt.

Jane, who is obviously sold on the possibilities of happiness in marriage, without hesitation evaluates the strengths of her own marriage. She also understands its periods of frustrations when she, like so many young mothers today, was trying to combine a home, children, and a demanding career.

She points out as a plus for the chances for her marriage being "eternally happy" the fact that she was 24 when she got married. She questions whether it is ideal to plan a career with a family in tow. As she says, "I don't think it's the ideal way to have a career. You've got the children as they come along, and the decisions after that have to be made really from the point of view of the family. That's why I didn't want to get married until I was 24. I had no intention of getting married earlier because I never could have done as much as I did.

"I was in all the plays by so many outstanding people like Somerset Maugham before I was married, but I was free to make career decisions then. 'Certainly I'll go on the road. Certainly I'll fly to Cleveland and be in that thing for a week.' There wasn't any question. Once you're married you can't make those decisions that way. You have to consider whether it is going to be right for everyone. Can I leave home and so forth? So, I really do feel that the single woman makes better decisions career-wise. Nevertheless, I'd say that at 24 my primary decision was to get married and be happy and live forever after with the man I loved."

Jane had just filmed "Lost Horizons" when she married, and she soon became pregnant. "I always tell my son that he's up there on the film when we did a retake and I'm in the wind and it's blowing and all. He's there. But then that next year I lost out on the momentum of my career for a couple of years. I did. I think now it's much easier to keep a career going."

In spite of Jane's conviction that it is not ideal career-wise to combine a career and young family, it is apparent that she never considered abandoning acting, which had from childhood been a part of her dreams and plans. She is a realist, and she doesn't attempt to conceal the conflict she experienced in her dual role. But she readily says that she was happy in her family life as she dealt with ambivalent emotions.

"I was disappointed that I wasn't getting on in my career and I was saying, 'I'll never work again and oh, I'm so unhappy. Oh dear, what's happening?' "

She remembers this frustration well but she also remembers her husband's help. She feels that his "very even disposition" helped keep her life in perspective. She also recalls the therapy of reading old press notices and realizing that she did have talent, and that there would be time to continue developing that talent later. She says, "I saw that in all these very distinguished plays by superb playwrites, I had always gotten marvelous notices. They said that I was 'the greatest,' and this or that or the other. And I realized that I might as well settle down and enjoy life and not be desperate to get on with my career at that moment. So I changed my attitude. I realized that I had done something already, and I had gotten somewhere, and then I just enjoyed my life as it developed from there on."

This decision to enjoy the days of child rearing and look forward to later opportunities for acting is part and parcel of Jane's no-nonsense personality.

She was the mother of two maturing sons and perhaps the time was exactly right for an opportunity such as "Father Knows Best" brought to her. This show which is still proving its popularity by its long run began in 1954. At that time Jane was living in New York, and she had just undergone two bad years in acting. Those were the years of the close of "Studio One" and other fine dramatic shows on television, and there was little opportunity for parts. She had been contacted several times, over the period of a couple of years, about doing the role of Margaret Anderson, but she didn't want to do what was at that time called a "serial."

Her agent sent a copy of a script, and she at first refused to read it until her husband suggested that she give it a try. She says that she was caught up in its warmth and its witty dialogue and decided to do a pilot, feeling that the chance of its going beyond the pilot stage was, as it always is in the industry, an open question. She did the pilot, and the rest is television history. The show became a part of American prime-time entertainment for the next six years.

Although the last episode was finished longer ago than she can even believe, she says that wherever she visits, whether in Hawaii or Europe, viewers still point and say with surprise, "Ah, yes, 'Father Knows Best.' "

Today Jane Wyatt is appearing on many popular television series, and she is particularly proud of a role in "Ladies of the Corridor" which allowed her to step outside her nice-mother image of Margaret Anderson. It permitted her to expand into what she describes as "a mean old lady who is terribly mean to her son." Such a new role allows Jane to stretch her wings farther, and Jane is a person who still likes to stretch vigorously.

While she is still doing many parts, she admits that she turns down many television roles which she feels are not what she really wants to do. With her firm realism, though, she says she will have to change her attitude again—because she is ready to cut out some of her other activities and get back to more acting. She says she is going to change her attitude of "I'd rather go fishing" when she is offered a script, or they just might stop offering her scripts.

Her work with the March of Dimes forms an impressive chapter in her life. She was the first woman member of the national foundation's board of trustees, and for many years she served as National Chairman of the Mother's March. She is very proud of the illustrious women who were her predecessors in this position. They are such truly remarkable women as Mary Pickford, Cornelia Otis Skinner, and Helen Hayes, as well as Beverly Sills whom she evaluates as the greatest Mother's March Chairman there has ever been.

She speaks of the aims of the March of Dimes with a great urgency which reveals her own concern for those with special problems. "One of the aims is to get rid of these teenage pregnancies; that's our biggest problem—children having children. They have them at thirteen, fourteen, fifteen years of age. A doctor speaking at a recent meeting said it was not at all unusual to have pregnant thirteen year olds come into his office. Their bodies aren't formed; they don't know what to do. They don't even know how to look after a doll, much less a baby.

"It's been very interesting to me that from the time I've been in the birth defects area we have moved back steadily in the child's experience. First, we were treating the birth-defect child after it was born. Then we moved back to the child in utero, and we did what we could do for the unborn and the mother. Then we got into prenatal care because so many girls come to the hospital, and they haven't been to any doctor previously, and here they are ready to deliver the baby. So we have prenatal care and we are urging the mothers to come for prenatal care, and are dealing with all the problems of getting them there. For example, we try to deal with the mother who already has children and who says she knows what to do, and who insists it is too difficult to go to the Doctor when there isn't anyone there to keep the children while she goes across the city to the clinic.

"We went through all of that, and now we've gone even farther back. Now we try to get information into the schools, to teach the adolescent girls of thirteen or fourteen years old how important it is to wait. I think that the administrators, the counselors, and the parents are derelict in that they have not set higher sights for these children, that they have not been able in some way to educate the children and stimulate them into other interests than going to bed with a boy and having a baby at thirteen."

Jane suddenly became philosophical as she looked beyond the early years for the young mother and said, "It makes life so long to get started so soon. Life is endless. We are all living longer and longer, and if you have the baby experience at thirteen, what have you got left?"

Jane's interest in young girls extended over into the area of couples living together without marriage. Her ideas were firm.

"I don't think much of it. I don't think it leads to marriage to begin with, and I don't think it leads to any kind of permanent relationship. It has so many other disadvantages, too. I was not domestically inclined, but I cannot imagine as a college student having to come home, cook the eggs, make the dinner, and all for this man that's also there. I cannot imagine having enough energy there to do so many things. When you go to college it's all *me, me, me*. It's *my* excitement, *my* world, *my* work, *my* thesis, and *my* play. I wouldn't have had the energy.

"But maybe I was just too self-centered. I was just too excited about what I was doing. And there wouldn't have been time to go and do the marketing; I really don't see how it works. I don't know why they want to do it. I don't think they are interested in going to college, but then again I always have to say that in my day you only went to college because you really wanted to and because you wanted to learn something. It wasn't that you got away from home and went to college. Now you graduate from school and the only question is what college are you going to? It is a little different, isn't it?"

It is apparent that Jane has thought a great deal about all aspects of rearing and encouraging children toward a better life, and she looks into her own life as a child and as a mother of two children to emphasize the need for giving children opportunities for early positive experience. She speaks of the joy of exposing children to museums, music, and theater, and then recalls her own childhood. She remembers seeing John Barrymore on the stage as Hamlet. She remembers a trip to Europe, as well as the day-by-day things which were just plain fun, the picnics and the books, as well as the joy of having her own horse.

She recalls especially that she, along with three siblings, was encouraged to be herself. She states well the principle of the need for a child having individual identity. "I think that my family managed to keep us separate. They used to tell me that I was not as beautiful as my sister, because she was a great belle, but that I had other things, and they specified the other things. With that kind of help a child can build up her own thing. I loved riding horses. In our family we all had our own thing that we did, and we were encouraged in that."

Beyond the facets of Jane's personality such as actress, charitable worker, wife, mother, and all-'round fine human being, there is a spiritual factor which springs from a depth which could not be expressed more effectively than from her own statement in a book. She says, "I have no desire to be a martyr but if I were put to the test to die or renounce my faith, I would die for Christ because there would simply be no other choice."[1]

Even her faith as a young girl was based on careful thought and appreciation of the person in whom she had placed her faith. She tells of a memory of how as a thirteen year old, "I suddenly found myself very hot and trembly and flushing bright red as I declared that if I were not convinced that Christ is the Son of God I would cease calling myself a Christian and become a Jew. I realized that if Christ is not the Son of God then the whole of the New Testament would be a lie of which the Catholic Church would be the continuation."[2]

Jane speaks of a deep feeling of association with the Old Testament and finds "it easy to share its longings and searchings and the distant memory of a better time. I often imagine that I have listened to Jeremiah; that I have wandered with Moses and that I was with Abraham in the Vale of Mambre."[3]

Jane knows exactly where she stands and she says in a way it is hard to forget, "Living just by convention is a bore but living for God is a challenge."[4]

The visit closed with Jane giving an overview of her life by trying to decide what period had been the happiest. "Sometimes I think right now is the happiest period in my life. But then, I think when I was in my thirties was the happiest time. I had a busy career and we had lots of parties to go to and we enjoyed them. We had lots of friends and we all seemed to have a lot of energy to spare and lots of excitement and things to do. It just seemed like a very nice time of my life, but I really think I'm happiest now. There's less pressure, for one thing. There's less pressure from a career viewpoint, I guess."

It does not seem at all unusual that Jane Wyatt is experiencing her happiest days now. She has her God, her family, her friends, and her work, but the real reason for her happiness is doubtlessly that skill, found in the attitude which is so apparent from the moment of meeting. It is a contentment deriving from some basic appreciation for life. This skill has enabled her to find a lifetime of happiness with her husband, and a lifetime of adjustment and balance of career and home. She doesn't maintain that it is all smooth or perfect—only that it is possible and after all worthwhile.

Perhaps Jane has something known as common sense; perhaps it is partially something known as acceptance of life as it truly is; and perhaps it is partially something known as faith that life is good. But whatever it is, it is basic to Jane, and it emanates from her in a wave of warm serenity. Life feels good and very satisfying when you visit with Jane Wyatt. Maybe that's one of the evidences of a good life.

---

1. Sheed, F. J. editor, *Born Catholics*. (New York and London: Sheed and Ward, 1954), p. 167.
2. Ibid., p. 168.
3. Ibid., p. 168.
4. Ibid., p. 170.

Lynda Jackson is the mother of two young daughters. She has returned to the university part time to complete her degree in journalism after experiencing the sad, but growth-inspiring, recovery from a divorce.

6. Lynda Jackson

Growth and Maturity from Divorce

"I think principally I've gained an appreciation of life. I've learned how to use my resources, learned to use what I have instead of thinking about what I might like to do. I'm going ahead and doing it and feeling superior and humble at the same time. Humble because there's so much to do in life and a little superior knowing that I can do a lot of the things."

Lynda Jackson is a very different person from the dependent, defenseless young woman she was three years ago. She has gained maturity and a sense of her own worth in her world, and she now sees herself as someone who can stand alone and deal with her life. She is one of the fortunate women who have gone through the pain of divorce and has come out stronger. It was not an easy experience, but now that the first terrible months are over she feels there is much satisfaction in weathering a night of disruptive and potentially destructive storm—to find a bright sunrise waiting at dawn.

She is tall and attractive with a flair for fashion. She wears her hair long and fluffed. She achieves a look of assurance in blue jeans or formal attire perhaps because, as she says, "I like to plan ahead about what I will wear, and then I can enjoy the occasion by feeling really well-dressed."

She looks back to evaluate her early view of herself by saying, "I've always had a very dramatic picture of myself, and perhaps this comes partially from the fact that I was an only child, and I grew up quite internalized in my thoughts. I have always been sure of myself and felt I could do anything I really wanted to do. I was willing to put effort into it and wait until it worked out, but I never doubted the outcome. For example, I

went to Chicago and I went to only one employment agency. I
sat there for five days until I took a job, and it was a very good
job. And it never occurred to me that I wouldn't get it, you
know. Because at that time I don't think it had occurred to me
that anyone would refuse me anything.

"I have never had fear about something that I had decided to
do. I would be more likely to have fears about relationships
with other people or something like that. But if it were something I thought was at all in my control, I wouldn't have fears.

"I think of myself as reserved but not shy, and I don't think
that I'm really easy to get to know deeply, but I can talk socially
with anyone about anything."

These all sound like positive statements which reflect a
vigorous approach to life. But as Lynda looks back to the
months, and even years, of her fourteen-year marriage to a
young man who was first a medical student, then an intern, a
resident, and still later in private practice as a surgeon, she
marvels that she was not vitally alive and participating in life.

"I could always be fairly satisfied by myself. I didn't have to
have a lot of people around me. We were so into the fact that
he was going to be the greatest doctor in the world, it was easy
for me to think that his training was the most important thing
for both of us. It didn't occur to me that I wasn't really doing
anything myself, because I so identified with him.

"But I was rather happy. I like to read and I was occupied,
but I don't think I was really alive. I was not myself. I was an extension of him. And that's what life was for me.

"I did have some interests and I worked at times. I always
knew that I wanted to write, and I wanted to do something with
writing. And I always had a sense of worth about myself.

"I wrote maybe sixty or eighty pages of a novel which I've
worked on again this year. The writing has always been a compulsion, but I had no realistic approach to it at that time. I had
no feeling that I would take something and sell it. That seemed
like a very remote experience for me to do something like that.

Even though I had worked for a publishing company and then as a journalist, I didn't see myself as a part of the publishing world. I don't think I was on the level of thinking that I am now. I don't think that I had a realistic approach to achievement since I lived very much inside myself.

"In fact, looking back I can hardly understand or explain that period of my life. It had an element of sleep-walking in it. I feel that I was lazy at that time, and I don't feel real good about myself in the period from the time I moved from Chicago to the time that I had my first child. I'm not sure to this day where my mind was because I think that my husband was doing just about all the thinking and contributing. I can't even remember what I was thinking about then; in fact memories are hazy for several years. I don't think I was with the rest of the world.

"I think I was fortunate there in Chicago that I had gotten such a good job with such a nice firm. But when we moved I was satisfied just to do temporary secretarial work. It seemed enough for me that he had the big career. And really that was foolish of me, but I just didn't know any better. I could have gone back to school and gone ahead and gotten my degree—I could have been spending my time much more usefully than I was. Why I didn't I really don't know. I guess I thought that I would do my grand, spectacular thing at some later time.

"It didn't occur to me to think that I should be pushing forward at the same time he was; I seem to have had no life at that period."

Lynda's first child was born in 1969, and she remembers this as one of the happiest and most exciting moments of her life. The baby was born the week the astronauts first walked on the moon, so she was named "Chandra," the Sanskrit word for "moon child."

Following Chandra's birth the family of three moved to Virginia where what Lynda terms "the less nice period" of her life followed.

She was diagnosed as having a blood disease which could

be fatal within a few months or maybe could be arrested. Lynda remembers this period of her life with such anguish that it is still hard for her to discuss details.

"I was actually very fortunate in the outcome, but I didn't know for two or three months which way it was going to be. There's nothing that can put you on your toes more than thinking you might not be around for very long. I had to go see a hematologist every week and have a blood sample taken, and at the same time I was pregnant. So it was a very, very trying experience. And then I had Nicole, my second daughter.

"When I became pregnant it was good for me because I had gotten this horrible death fear out of my head while concentrating on her. But then after I had her, this fear of dying came back again.

"I don't think this period either brought our marriage closer or put it farther apart. It goes so deep that I really can't talk about it. I spent all the time with the children that I could, and my husband encouraged me to because we didn't know how long I had. It was just a thing that was there, and I can only say that I was very fortunate with the way it all came out.

"I never had a feeling of great elation over my recovery because it was a gradual thing that the doctors kept watching all the time. So, I never could really believe it was over, and I can't to this day really feel that everything is alright."

Several years of apparently normal family life passed, and Lynda's husband completed his training and went into practice. Together they bought a new home, complete with swimming pool and an acre of lawn. It was located close to excellent schools for the children, but as Lynda says, "I had a terrible sense of foreboding about it. Things just were not right, and then my husband came in and told me that it was over. It was so strange, really, but I don't think you can ever blame any one person or one event when things like this occur. It's usually the culmination of a lot of things in your time together. You don't see it at the time, but it's true. I think that we probably had not been happy for a long time.

"He was thirty-six, and I think he had finally just gotten to the point in his life where he was really beginning to think about something other than study. The practice he set up for himself was beginning to go, and he had finally gotten to the point where there wasn't something on his back every minute."

Lynda can now talk calmly of the night her husband left. Even though he had actually left at her insistence, she did not really want him to go.

"I made several desperate telephone calls to his office. All I could think about when he first left was getting him back. I think that would probably be the normal reaction. That seemed like the most immediate thing. I can remember such unreal days followed. Then I remember about a week later I rearranged the furniture, which is one of my therapeutic things. I rearrange my house. Then I sat down, and there was some television show on the girls and I all liked. And I had just rearranged, not only my furniture but my life, I felt.

"We all three sat down on the sofa together and ate ice cream while we watched this favorite television show. I looked around and thought, *well, this isn't so bad, is it?* And that was my first good response. I didn't realize it then, but I think it fleetingly went through my mind that the world had not, after all, suddenly come to an end and fallen off its axis. But, of course, it was not over at that point. I think that about forty-five minutes later the telephone rang, and he and I had another huge argument on the phone.

"But it was about a week later that I did the normal things. I went for eight or ten days and didn't eat, which was good for my figure but not good for my mind. I sobbed and cried and became a complete martyr and went through all the phases I think everyone probably goes through. But it did occur to me a few times that the world hadn't really ended."

Lynda returned to the image of rearranging the furniture since this seemed some way to typify the events of her life at that moment.

"I wanted to tell you about moving the furniture around

because I saw a parallel in it, and I was thinking the other day that this is what you really start to do when you begin to live for yourself. You rearrange things in your mind to fit what you're doing that day or that week, and it doesn't stay permanently. You begin to realize that things do not stay the same, and that's not necessarily bad. Sometimes you have to rearrange every piece of furniture, even the heavy ones you thought were settled in one place. I find the ideas in my life are really no different from the way they probably were when I was eight or ten years old, but I rearrange the ideas to suit the way I feel now. I have to adapt them to reality, to what is really happening.

"During the next three months or so my attitude was sometimes on the mountain, and then in a valley, and half up the mountain, and back in a valley. And all through that I made some conscious decisions.

"For one thing I began to have a bit more appreciation for myself and what I could handle. Then I decided that I was not going to permit myself to be bitter. I had had other friends who were so bitter that it was disgusting to listen to them talk. I didn't want to hate that way. I felt that would be demeaning to me. I'm a contradiction because I did have a tendency to put myself down and blame myself at that stage, but I also valued myself a great deal, and I didn't want to do anything that was beneath me. To me it would be demeaning to be bitter.

"I also decided that I would not let this experience destroy my illusions about life. I wouldn't let it destroy my anticipation that idealistic and romantic events were still waiting for me around the corner. And of course, I had so much to keep me going. I had two beautiful little girls. I also made a decision about them. I made a decision that I would not, even though they're the most important thing in my life, be an albatross around their necks, that I would not be a parasite on them. It's very difficult not to play the role of the martyr, taking care of two beautiful children when your husband has left you after fourteen years. I tried very hard to keep from getting into that game."

It is much easier to make statements than to live up to them, and Lynda found that she had to develop techniques for getting through certain events, periods of sadness, or sudden memories. Some of the techniques were so small, others larger.

"One important thing was that I had lost some weight again. I liked to look at myself in the mirror and realize that I did, in fact, look very good.

"I also started reading some of the self-help books that helped me see myself advancing through various stages of shock, and then accepting the fact that things had happened to me, but I was still a worthwhile person.

"I didn't sit down and read the Bible, but I did read brief devotions, and they gave me a lift.

"It's strange, so many people told me they were encouraged by reading of other people's divorces, but it didn't strike me that way. I think if a person is starving it is not helpful to see other people who are also desperately hungry. I didn't read a lot of books about women who had gone through a divorce. I really didn't care what their situation was.

"My mother and dad were very supportive. I realize that you have a feeling all the time you're growing up, that you must protect your loved ones from any bad things that have happened to you, as if they have never had any experiences. They were very helpful about letting me express myself, and they were very warm and didn't say, 'Oh, this is so terrible.'

"Also, since I am a writer, I took a writing approach to grief. But really I think this would be helpful to anyone, since writing helps you put your thoughts in order and recognize the small steps you are making toward recovery.

"I'd done this all my life, and I found it helpful to sit down and write out some of my thoughts. This is the way I did get rid of some of the bitterness. You can't sit around saying or telling other people all the time that someone else is a so and so—I mean it gets old and nobody wants to hear it after awhile. You don't even want to hear it yourself. I did have a situation where my husband was seeing the children back and forth all the time. So I had to see him, and this was not something that I could walk off and leave, and I can't now. So I had to deal with it in some way. I did find that I could deal with the bitterness of such events in a sad little poem. Then the poem held the bitterness and my mind was free. This is one I wrote."

Return

They are coming home soon
The door will open
They will laugh and smile at Mommy
Warm, eager, and glad

I will take two little hands
While I squeeze in the tears
Because he cannot stay
And there is nothing left to say

"I found myself seeking out old friends. I felt after my separation that I enjoyed being around couples that were happy. I didn't necessarily want to hear another person's problems. I had enough problems without really hearing someone else's. But it was funny. I heard more things then I had ever heard. People confessed things and told me things from families to friends to children. They really had never been so open with me before, and I've wondered since if people feel you are more vulnerable when you've had a problem and they feel more open towards you. I don't really know why they feel so open with you. Perhaps when you have had something happen to you like that, you are more sensitive to other people, and they sense that you have come out of the cocoon of your own little existence into a universal world of grief.

"Strange, I found myself being very sensitive to my surroundings. I found in that first few months after my separation that everything was more intense to me from physical to mental things. I was just more aware of everything that was going on. It was almost as if I had a new set of sensors. Colors and tastes were more intense, and things that people said came through to me so vividly that at times I was almost overcome with the widsom and perceptiveness of chance remarks.

"And speaking of remarks people make, I think talking and having someone listen was probably my best therapy. I think being able to say things without worrying about how they sounded was the biggest help. I could tell how I sat out by the pool and felt relief from all the grief for a few minutes, and I didn't worry about it sounding silly or theatrical. I could just say it. I think communicating with one special friend all along the way may have been my best therapy. Her ears were my biggest relief.

"I had begun to mend a little when Christmas came. But I think the psychiatrists all tell us our worst times are vacations and holidays. Of course, our first Christmas experience was bad because with the children so young, we had always made a great thing of lots of decorations in our home with Santa Claus, and the family in for a visit. The way we worked it out that first Christmas was my husband came over that evening, and we prepared all of their Santa Claus things. He stayed through the night, stayed that morning, and saw them get their presents. Then the children and I left for my parents' home. This was very difficult, and I felt that I had to keep reassuring them that he still loved them, but I think all of that is partially reassuring yourself that maybe somebody still loves you. You know, you put your emotions on other people.

"For some reason throughout my life Christmas has always been something that I've anticipated very much, and I think I could almost equate it with marriage, a woman anticipating getting married and thinking that it's going to be this perfect situation. And maybe the honeymoon is Christmas Eve while your wedding is when the packages are to be opened the next morning. But it doesn't always turn out that way. Down deep I was grieving and thinking that this Christmas was not going to be a perfect and glorious experience, and suddenly a very sane thought struck me. I realized that all those other Christmases had been partially good and partially bad. I had been overworked at times, rushed to death, dissatisfied with plans, and so forth, and suddenly I knew that this was just a Christmas like the others. It was good and it was bad, and that was a sobering thought."

We wondered if Lynda felt her thoughts paralleled her husband's, and she answered with what again indicated a carefully considered decision. "I've gotten to the point in the last few months of taking good advice from some friends. That is, not to think about or try to imagine what his thoughts are about anything. A woman that's divorced, if she's truly divorced, has to get to the place where she no longer worries about that person's emotions and what might happen to him emotionally. That is no longer a part of her life."

Lynda had the added responsibility of explaining the divorce to her children. She feels that this was one of the most difficult jobs she had to face. "It was very difficult the first evening because it was such a shock to me. I just hardly knew what had happened. It seemed that I had to say over and over again, 'Your Daddy and I decided that we didn't want to live together.' I didn't want to say he decided. I didn't want to lay all the blame on him.

"There were several times when I couldn't keep from crying in front of them, even though I tried not to. They may have heard us two or three times have some sort of an argument, and they certainly overheard telephone conversations. I mean, there are some things that are inevitable. I think the older child resented and still does to a certain extent, but she's confused about who to resent and what to resent. I tried fairly hard to tell them that it was certainly not anything they had done. That seemed to me the most important thing for them to know— that it was certainly nothing they had done to bring this about.

"I felt very bad as the divorce proceedings dragged on. This may sound a little dramatic, but I thought of the day of the divorce as 'D Day,' and I kept thinking of myself as a horse with a broken leg just waiting to be shot. I felt that what had happened as a horrible nightmare nine months before was going to be a reality.

"I took off my rings and I wrote a poem about that day, and that seemed to help a little.

Definite Action

I took them off,
Your rings.
Where they were
An impression remains.

"I can honestly say that I never consciously anticipated anything like this happening to me. Yet in my mind all the time, when I was not feeling fully alive, there was something inside, a sixth sense, telling me that at one time in my life I would be living differently. I can't explain it. It was not really a conscious thing, but it seemed there was something there saying, someday you'll be doing other things; this is a waiting period. And yet when this particular thing came about I was shocked."

Lynda says without hesitation that she likes herself much better now than she did earlier. She enumerates what she has gained.

"I think principally I've gained an appreciation of life. I've learned how to use my resources, learned to use what I have instead of thinking about what I might like to do. I'm going ahead and doing it and feeling superior and humble at the same time. Humble because there's so much to do in life, and a little superior knowing that I can do a lot of those things.

"Surprisingly, I must say that it took grief to wake me up. Experiencing all the depression has taught me a number of things. I have finally gotten to the point that I can see a pattern in the depression. The first two or three months were very bad. Then I made a trip to New Orleans with some friends, and that broke the pattern for me. After that I began to see that I was attractive to other people, including men, and the depression became less.

"And just recently, when I felt I was all through the thing, I realized I had the idea that you would reach a certain stage and then you would 'live happily ever after.' I still believed that; even after being separated I thought I would just go through so many things, and I would reach one point, and everything would be perfect, and I would never have any more problems. I really couldn't get it through my head that that wasn't the way it was. And I'd begun to realize recently that the aim was not getting all your problems solved, but rather it's reaching a level where you can handle them as they come along. And I think that has lifted my depression and given me a clear outlook.

"I sometimes wonder if that statement about 'living happily ever after' is something we pick up from the ending of every good children's story. Actually, it's so foolish because the only way that would ever be possible is in death, because life is not static.

"And I think this is not a feminine delusion. I think men have the same idea in their heads, even though they say men and women are really so different. They reach their goal in their career or whatever, and they think, *Well now, I've done everything or I've gotten to this particular level, and I will live happily ever after.* But that doesn't work for them, either. They think that finding the ideal woman and reaching this level is the beautiful ending, but the whole line of thought is a great error for men or women.

"I kept discovering new remedies for depression, and maybe

most people need these throughout life to some degree, even if they are not experiencing a divorce or other disaster. I slept for a month or two after I was first separated, and I hated to wake up. Sleep was an escape. Then I went through a period where I stayed awake all the time and couldn't sleep. But now as I've gone along, all this has smoothed out and I find little depression remedies correct most of the downs.

"Sometimes it's rearranging the furniture or it's sitting down and writing a poem. It may be talking to a friend on the phone, or taking your little girl out and buying her a new pair of shoes, or going into the kitchen and cooking something, or getting in the car and going out to the movies. The main thing all of us have to realize is: it's not good to enjoy your depression because that's kind of a trap. Depression is something that's very real, and you do have to fight it, whether you have any horrible experience or not. But I think just getting the energy up to fight it is important. It's like having to sit down and write out your bills; you don't want to do that; it takes a long time. It's a boring little task, and it's also boring to fight depression, but you do have to try to make some effort to fight it and not sit and wallow in it. Maybe once in awhile you can read sad books and listen to sad music. Sometimes I do that; a few times I've just let myself go ahead and cry, and get that out of my system, but not frequently."

Lynda has thought and evaluated for three years. Now life is coming together for her, she feels, realistically and with interest.

She says, "I'm beginning to live close to my dream although there are lots of things I can dream of improving. I would like to remarry eventually, but I'm in no hurry. I would want to marry someone who is a whole person, not someone who has no problems but someone who has a good grip on life.

"I am back at the university, and I think getting that degree in journalism will be a great shot in the arm. I am teaching creative writing to a group of children, and I'm helping edit a book. I have completed one novel but have not found a publisher, and I am working on another novel. I'm a member of Authors Unltd. of Houston, and that is a source of constant encouragement. I date some and I think this brings a certain needed excitement to life. I feel quite serene most of the time.

"I feel a great responsibility to rear my childen well, and I work very hard at that. I'm teaching my girls that if they want to get married when they're even as young as eighteen years old that's fine, but they're going to continue going to school, and they're going to be doing something. I think, regardless, I'm going to see to it that they keep themselves, their bodies, and their minds alive and attractive at all times. I just think that the children know so much more today, and not just about sex, but they're just more aware about everything. And I think that especially ten years from now, they will not be satisfied, or think in terms of just getting married and doing nothing else.

"I think a man and a woman loving each other has got to be the most wonderful experience in the world, but I think they will realize that they can add more to that experience by being whole people themselves. By being whole in this context I mean being alert and alive and enthusiastic about life and pursuing goals—not selfishly but realistically—because we were put on earth to do something with ourselves and not ever to be just an extension of someone else.

"I've come through a bad experience, but I've learned a lot and even reached the place where I can write a poem and call it 'Final Act,' and maybe that says something about where I am now.

Final Act

What is love
You think I
Do not know?

Maybe love
Is simply
Letting go.

Letting go
Letting go
Letting go.

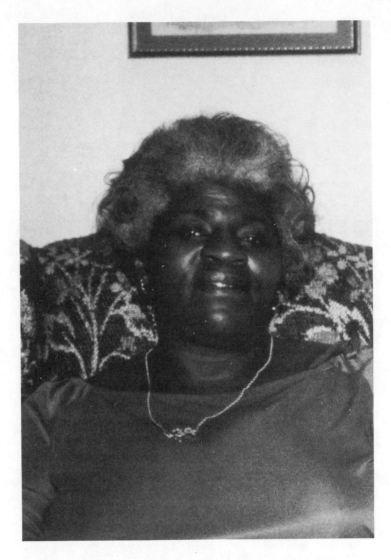

Ann Campbell is the mother of NFL rushing star, Earl Campbell, as well as ten other children. She reared the children alone, but she has shared with the world the acclaim for her son and her own entrance into a new vista of national recognition.

7. Ann Campbell

A Champion in Her Own Right, Mother of NFL Star, Earl Campbell

"Just looking back on life, it has been rough. But then it has been good too. And when I think about it, it has been a lot of fun all along the way."

It is a long way from the rose fields in Tyler, where the Texas wind sings of open fields, to the Grand Ballroom of the New York Hilton, where the microphones crackled with the announcement that Earl Campbell had just won the Heisman Trophy for 1977.

The distance from Tyler to New York has been more than the geography of space for Ann; it has been the geography of change in life pattern, but only in some specific areas. For in the areas of responsibility, hard work, and worship, there must be for Ann no change. These are the areas which she knows are right for her. These are not available to the changing touch of sudden fame or money for these are realities, and she has grown up with them as old and true friends.

When we first met Ann, the day was cold and biting, but she extended her arms slowly to take in her warm house where the gas heater glowed brightly. Her voice was rich with contentment as she said, "This is what the Lord has given me and this is where I live."

We could see around the corner to the bedroom where her eleven children had slept, and where her mother had died, at the age of eighty-six, surrounded by grandchildren who took her for rides in her wheelchair on summer afternoons.

We understood her contentment as she told us her story of struggles and victories over problems. We saw why Earl Campbell's honors were recognized by Ann as only one more of the good things straight from the hand of God. They were like the rose fields on one side of the little house where she has spent her adult life and the new house Earl is having built for her nearby. They are evidence of her conviction that God is giving her more good things than she can find either time or energy to use.

She has so much, she feels, that she can agree with Earl's statement that if the Lord calls him home tomorrow he won't complain because he has already had one wonderful life.

She began to talk of the football game which Earl had played the previous night. She said, "It seems he played the best that I've seen him play since he's started for the Oilers. I felt real good going into the game. I just felt like they would win, and I don't know why, because I'm always a little bit pessimistic about football because you never know. It's a funny game. In minutes you can lose and in minutes you can win. But somehow or the other I just had a feeling that the Oilers were going to take them on pretty good last night.

"Earl called after the game. He called and wanted to know, 'Momma, are you watching?' I said, 'yes.' He said, 'Did you see me when I said, 'Hi Mom'? I said, 'I sure did. What happened to you?' and he said, 'Well, the whole team was just giving tonight.' "

Ann has watched Earl and his brothers play football so long and so often that the game and the players' actions in the game are no mysteries. The games are entertainment, but much more; they are a field of work, like farming or teaching, and they are an opportunity for the boys to present themselves as modest and honorable men before the world. She is proud of Earl's modesty which is seen in his unfailing sharing of the limelight with his team members. She is proud that "he says very little about himself."

She worries too. She was worried because it looked like he

was limping. She had told him the night before, "Well, I thought I saw you crippling off the field there a little bit." He said, "Aw, I just hopped off the field."

These were the shared words of a mother and son while the crowd was still screaming after the victory in the Astrodome.

She has also noticed with other football enthusiasts that Earl just drops the ball quietly, even gently, to the turf after making a touchdown. There is none of the so familiar wild victory dance.

She has noticed, and she says, "He's just real modest with it. It makes you wonder about him sometimes. You see them sometimes when they make a touchdown, they throw the ball and they jump up and down; but Earl doesn't. He's never done that even much in high school. He was just calm like he is now. This is just his life. This is the way he's been. He's kinda like Coach Phillips said last night, he just kinda likes to take it easy and be quiet."

The nights Earl's games are televised are big nights in the little frame house. It fills up with relatives until the sofa and floor are covered. They yell encouragement to Earl's running form on the screen until Ann gets her little black-and-white set and takes it back to her bedroom. But that doesn't mean things stay quiet, she insists. Until the game is over there is someone running back and forth to shout, "Did you see that, Momma?" or "He's really going tonight."

But Earl is only one of Ann's eleven children, and she is quick to express her equal pride in all the family. With all the publicity about Earl, we were surprised to hear her say, "Herbert was as good a football player as Earl or better, I understand from a lot of the coaches. But the school wasn't integrated, and he didn't get the publicity Earl got. But I understand that Herbert was as good a lineman as Earl is a back. When he finished school, it was shortly after his Daddy died. I had all those small children, and I just really didn't seek and look into it. Herbert went to college one semester and he got discouraged.

"But Earl is doing what he has always wanted to do. When he says this is his God-given talent, I believe he is right. You know, he never could bring up his other work here on the farm. He just wasn't as good a worker. He was there with the rest of them, but he just couldn't bring it up. He never objected because he knew he had to work. But I just really believe football is what the Lord had cut out for him. Now my twins have always talked of going to school under the football scholarship, but they wanted to become coaches. They never have cared about playing ball. And they never talked too much about professional ball."

Ann was eager to talk of the present status of the other children. Two of the boys are in Austin playing football at the University of Texas, one is in Germany, Earl is in Houston, and the rest are in Tyler. It is a close family that still works together in the roses, talks things over, and relies heavily on each other.

Ann was chuckling about a phone call she had just received from her daughter in Germany.

"Guess what she wanted?" she laughed. "She wanted my turkey dressing recipe, and she wanted my other daughter's lemon pie recipe. She could have written and asked."

Some of Ann's children are still at home. Her youngest child is sixteen and a grandson, Victor, who spends time with her came in from kindergarten bringing a picture of a Thanksgiving turkey with a crayoned tail as bright as any peacock's.

We had read Earl's statement that any woman who had done what his mother had done deserved a crown. We had also, along with a nation of footbell viewers, seen his television message of greeting and assurance that he was not hurt expressed to his mother each time he was interviewed after a game.

Exactly what had she done that left such a vivid stamp on the minds of her children? She had held them all, all eleven of them, together after her husband's death, and she had given them the assurance that they would be together. There was no question here, no vacillating—she let them know it would be hard, but she also let them know that the future of the family was secure. Ann Campbell never questioned the fact.

"My husband died kinda sudden," Ann says. "He got sick about a week; he was in the hospital getting ready to go to another hospital in Shreveport and he had a heart attack. He died on the seventh day of May in 1966."

She remembers the circumstances vividly. "I tell you for one thing I really was down in the dumps, because at that point I knew the Lord, but not like I do now. I really didn't think I would be able to manage eleven children. But it would be real hard for anybody to make me believe you can't do a thing if you try.

"A lot of times I tell my children, when they tell me they can't do somethng, 'You can. What if I had said I couldn't when your Daddy died? Just folded it up and said I just can't?' But if you make one step, the Lord will make two, and if somebody sees you trying they'll help you. It would be hard for me to say that you can't do a thing, but you can't unless you try."

She remembers her emotions on that day years ago. "It's strange, but right then I really didn't have time to grieve, but now every once in a while it comes down. You know what I mean? I think about him. But not then really because I never wanted my children to feel that I was grieving. And a lot of times I'd be sitting there, wouldn't be saying anything, and they'd want to know what's wrong with me. And I told them nothing was wrong because I wanted them to be happy.

"But it had all been such a shock. That day we got up at 7 in the morning, and he went to the bath. I asked him, 'You know you're going for treatment at 9. Do you want me to go?' and he said, 'No. I'd rather you stayed here with the kids.' And I just didn't know that he was that near to dying. I knew he was out of breath, perspiration was on his face, and I went to the bathroom with him. We walked back and just as he went to get up on the bed, well, something hit him, and I could tell he was dead by the time his head touched the pillow.

"The next few days are a blur in my mind, but I do remember this: one of the deacons at the church asked me if I would mind if he would 'lift' an offering for me and my children that day at the church. And I said, 'Well, no, I wouldn't mind it.' And he put a plate down and as people viewed his body they put money on that table. And they took up about $360 that day. And I had that money to live on until I got my Social Security started, and the children got out of school and began work.

"The children did pretty well about it all. They just kind of handled it themselves. Now I'll tell you what Earl said about it when I came home that day from the hospital. My brother brought me home, and they were all sitting around on the porch and wanting to know had their dad really died. I said, 'Yes,' and I was crying and my daughter was on the bed crying. And Earl said to me, 'Well, Momma, since this just had to be, then let's just have the funeral as quick as possible and get everything over with and get settled down again.' And I won't ever forget that.

"I was forty-five years old when this all happened, and I had ten children to support since only one was out of school."

Lacking education, after Ann became a widow, she worked in homes and went on growing roses. "I could always go to the bank and borrow a little money to help operate the rose fields. We still operate the fields and we have about thirty thousand bushes now, and we sell a lot of them dry root while they are dormant."

In the early days after being widowed, Ann talked to the children about the ways they could help in the rose fields. Somehow it was hard for us to think of Earl as a worker in the roses, when we were so accustomed to seeing his football-helmeted face on our television screens, but we sensed that the roses are far more than mere flowers or mere labor in Ann's mind. They are also the hallmark of her city, Tyler, which has been so good to her and which gave Earl the nickname of the "Tyler Rose" somewhere along his career. Roses are a crop and a science and they are also financial security. They have been a part of the life of her family.

She remembers one discussion when she had to tell the children that she could not make the living for them by herself.

"My children knew that. I set them down after their Daddy was funeralized and the family all went home, and we were sitting here on the porch on Saturday afternoon. They were all around me and we just talked about it. I told them, 'I'll feed you, I'll put clothes on your back, but you must help work. I cannot make it by myself.' And I meant that, and I've never taken it back. A lot of evenings my children would come home from school and they would go the the neighbors and work in the afternoons. And when they worked, everybody brought their money to me. I helped manage that and then they'd always say, 'Well, Momma, after you buy groceries or after you pay your bill, we want a couple of dollars.'

"I never had problems. I've always been able to manage with what we made. I told them too that in this family we would do alright as long as everybody didn't make trouble, so we wouldn't have to carry the money down to pay fines. I said that we aren't going to do that. The one that makes trouble is just going to have to get out of it the best way he can, because it's not fair to the rest of them to take what's made and carry it down to the court house to get out of jail. I never had that type of problem either.

"Another thing is, there's something I never will forget that my dad taught his boys. That was that an idle mind is the devil's workshop, and I really believe that. My children knew when they came home from school that they had something to do. And I certainly believe a child that's walking around and doing nothing has nothing to think about but getting into trouble."

We wondered how Ann's philosophy could be applied in an urban situation where jobs are hard to find and there are no rose fields to offer ready employment. We asked her what children could do if they lived in Chicago or perhaps

Philadelphia. Her answer was not hopeful.

"There wouldn't be anything to do. But I tell you I have been questioned by my children about working while the other kids were walking around not doing anything, but I told them that our family worked.

"The bus used to get through here around 4:10 when football practice wasn't going on, and they worked for the neighbors from about 4:10 until maybe 7:00 when they couldn't see, making extra money. And then they'd come home and get their lessons for school. Working in the roses is kind of a seasonal thing and holidays like Easter, my children worked in the fields. They usually wanted something in the clothes line. I never will forget they were out for Easter and they budded roses. At that time they were getting about fifteen dollars a thousand buds, and they made enough to buy three suits. That was a suit for Earl and a suit for the twins. The work was good for them and they enjoyed their new suits. I believe that kids who don't have anything to do are sure to be in trouble."

As Ann talked, we were overcome with the awesome thought of attempting to support ten children, some of them little more than babies. We wondered if there was any way this task could have been cushioned by earlier preparation. We asked Ann and she told us with a certain sadness of what is probably the one regret of her life. It was her missed opportunity to attend college. Her story was the same one we had heard from so many other women who said in varying words, "If I had just realized what was possible, I could have done something differently."

Ann told of the days during World War II when she finished high school in the spring and married in June. She remembers high school with pleasure as she says, "I loved school and would have gone on to college if I'd used my head right."

She recalls that in those days most parents had little education and didn't think of sending children to college. But the possibility of college following her graduation is clear in Ann's mind. "My husband was in the service, and I didn't have any children until he was out. He was in the service for four years because he put in two years in France, and at that time I could have gone to Texas College and got a degree, but I didn't. I went to work in a laundry instead."

The vivid reality of her missed opportunity is apparent as she says without question that she would have studied home economics, and that she would have used her degree to teach. She sees home economics as an important area for young women, perhaps the most important, as she explains, "I would tell young women today that if they are married to really base their whole lives around their homes. Now I don't mean not to have any activities, but to stay close to home and take care of their home and children. This would be the best advice I could give them."

Ann feels that the church's influence in her children's lives has been a real force, but she also feels that it has been her responsibility to see that the children get to church.

"We got up here on Sunday morning and went to church. And I had them to understand we will be in somebody's church service every Sunday morning. I would tell them, 'You're not there very long, and you have all afternoon to ride your horses and play ball, but if you go to church you might hear something that will keep you from doing something drastic before the day is gone.' We went to church right along. My husband had it going when he died and I kept it going."

We wondered if the children had ever rebelled and refused to go, but Ann assured us that it was only on special occasions that the children resisted.

"The only time that I ever had any objections to it was when they started playing football and sometimes they'd be tired, but I'd make them get up and go to church. I said, 'If you can go to football games, you can go to church.' So, we'd get up and go. Earl used to teach and he used to be superintendent of Sunday School. They all sang in the junior choir until they grew out of it, and then the boys joined the male chorus. And I've got four kids singing in the male chorus at our church now.

"We go to most of the services at the Hopewell Baptist Church, I used to make Sunday School every Sunday morning but since I've grown older and got pretty feeble and feel bad a lot of Sundays, I mostly make the 11 o'clock service, and sometimes I go to prayer service on Wednesday night. I joined that church in my childhood days, and I've been there all of my life. So if anybody knows anybody, I know these people.

"I would say that the most important thing about being in church service is that it has really helped me to motivate my children to be Christians and know how to treat other people. I have always taught them to respect the rights of other people. Don't ever feel like they're the whole show. Always see the other side."

Ann told how they were able to buy a car when the boys were young, and we immediately had visions of the squabbles among the boys for the use of the car. But Ann put our minds at rest. She said, "We never had that problem. I did the driving, you know."

We all laughed together at the picture of Ann at the wheel as chauffeur for her large family and she chuckled with us. "I used to take the boys to see their girl friends, drop them off, and they called me at night and I'd go pick them up. I knew that I couldn't get insurance for those young boys to drive the car so I did the driving for a long, long time."

Sitting beside Ann before her cozy fire it was hard to recall the racial problems that had burned through the country in the sixties, but we realized that those were the years when Ann was rearing most of her seven boys and four girls, so we wanted to know whether they had experienced racial problems. She was quick to say that they had tried to stay out of disturbances.

"My children just get along with people. We just haven't had a whole lot of problems. I guess they're teaching my children about the rights of other people at school, and I taught them at home. And I can tell you this one thing. The night they had 'Earl Campbell Day' here, the night they had the banquet, there were as many whites there as blacks. And I really believe everybody there was sensitive. I don't believe anybody was there just to be there. I believe they really meant to honor Earl."

The night before at dinner someone had said that Tyler loves Earl Campbell. It was such a warm, open statement that I repeated it to Ann and asked how she felt about it.

Her enthusiasm lighted her eyes and her face as she said, "Well, I just believe that's true. Now I don't know who made the statement, but I believe it. And the reason I say I believe it's true because that's the way I am. I just love people and I have as many white friends, I guess, as I do black. And then I know I got lots of them through Earl's success. And everybody that I've ever come in contact with through Earl is a joy. And would you believe a man called me from Honolulu last night? He said, 'Mrs. Campbell, this is your friend from Honolulu.' I said, 'You don't mean you saw the game over there?' We have friends of all races all over the country now, and I am just happy to know that the Lord has let me live here to see the white and the black get together, because there's not going to be any separation when we leave down here."

Ann's conviction that racial problems are being improved was so apparent that we pressed her for a prophesy of the future. What, in fact, would be the situation between the races in the year 2000?

She was very thoughtful as she answered.

"Well, the devil's at work down here but I feel like this. If Christians can outman him and outdo him, there won't be any difference in people when the time comes. I just feel like before the end of time we'll be as one. Now that might be a lot for an uneducated woman to be saying, but now that is just my feeling about it. I might be wrong. Maybe one reason I feel kind about the races is that my mother and daddy were very kind people, and I was raised that way. I never saw much reason to be hard and harsh. I never did see any reason to be harsh when I was raising the children."

She talked about disciplining children in kindness as she said, "Well, I want to tell you. I never have been a type of person to use the belt. I've talked to the children, you know, and I guess my talking was the belt. But I never have been a type of person to just get one and hold him down, you know. It would just do something to me. I'd just be upset. Now understand, I have not raised my children without having to whip them. But I have done everything else I could by talking to them to try to keep from doing it. I don't think I ever have had to punish my children very much. We never had that type of problem."

The good family is the answer! This is the message that works in and out of Ann Campbell's conversation. And she is not thinking only of parents and children. She is thinking of the extended family, of her mother and her aunts who have lived out their lives in her house and in trailer homes on her fourteen inherited acres.

They were all close until they died, sharing their final illnesses as they had shared their good times.

"My mother died right here in my home. In my back bedroom, back there where I sleep. She died at eighty-six years old. She lived in the corner house there, she and my sister and her three children. Her house burned and my mother and my sister got burned. But when they got over their burns, when they could come out of the hospital, I moved them here. Fourteen people stayed right here in this particular house, me and all my children, my mother and my sister and her three children. After my mother died, my sister got the trailer home over there, but we lost her two years ago. We had been real close, real close."

We looked around the house with its six rather small rooms, and we asked Ann how she could put fourteen people into this space. But it was no problem to her. Quickly she told us where the beds were placed and where her bed had been in the hall where she could care for her mother if she called in the night. She said with pride, "I gave up my bed to my mom, and I slept there on a half-bed."

She went on to tell of the family's cooperation, of how she shared the work of caring for the sick with other family members.

She told how her sister worked during the day and helped at night and how the children "pitched in" when they came home. With great contentment she remembered, "My mother was never lonely; she never spent a lonely day here or a lonely night by herself. There was always somebody with her."

She is familiar with rest homes for the aged and ill, but her feelings about them are ambivalent.

"I can't hardly put it together," she says. "I really don't like the idea much. I think as long as you can keep your parents, you should. Now that's my idea about it. Sometimes they get in a condition that you can't. But I haven't experienced it, and there's just not too much I can say about it because we kept mom. She would slide down in the bed, you know, but I have so much family here the boys could get her and put their arms around her and pull her back up on her pillow. We didn't even have a lot of lifting to do.

"But all families are not like my family, so there's not too much comparison that I can make because I've never had it to go through with. We had all the children and they loved her so well. In the summer time we would put her in her wheel chair and they would take her and just roll her around and around the house. I think it is just very important to have your family real close. It's really nice to have big families and keep the closeness to you.

"Now our young people are getting so smart they think a big family is the worst thing you could have. Most children do. They've gone out on these pills, and having tubes tied, and all that type of thing, and it's just kind of hard for me to say that they're right. I feel like this—if you are blessed with the children, you're going to make it. The Lord is going to put more blessings there than you are able to enjoy. Do you know that's true? I used to hear my parents say this, and I just wondered what they were talking about. How can the Lord bless you with more than you are able to enjoy? That has happened to me. He has already blessed me with more than sometimes I'm able to enjoy. Earl gave me a brand-new car, and that car sits there; I don't even feel like going anywhere. That's more than I'm able to enjoy."

Ann is now surrounded by her loving grown children and her responsibilities are lighter. She knows the gratification of a good life's work almost completed, but we wondered if she had always been so convinced of the joys of being the mother of a big family. We asked if she had felt such satisfaction when the children were young and the babies were crying, or had she felt resentment then? She didn't have to consider the answer.

"Never did," she said. "My mother was the motherly type and when I was playing with the little girls, I used to say, 'I'm going to be just like my mom. I'm going to have eleven children.' But I didn't really mean that, but after being blessed with the children, I have just thoroughly enjoyed it. I've done everything I could do to cook and feed them and keep clothes on their backs. As God would have it, somebody was always nice, giving me something. And my children never created chaos. They'd always wear what we had. I never had problems with my kids about clothes.

"I know it helped that I had a good husband. I tell people now that when I was having those babies he'd say, 'Aw wife, you don't know what you might have one day.' And I think about it now, and I imagine he'd turn over in his grave if he could see how the children have grown up and how I'd got to go to New York to see Earl get the Heisman. I never had an idea that anything like that would happen to me. And I got the 'Mother of the Year Award' in Tyler and the 'Married Mother of the Year Award' in Austin."

We had to mention the presence of the house under construction across the yard; Ann had not acknowledged its presence in our conversation. Perhaps she felt it would not be modest to point out something so fine which was hers. But once we had spoken of it she was quick to tell of the good things she looked forward to.

There was the fireplace which would burn the logs the boys brought in from their own woods here on their land. There were the walk-in closets, and most of all there was the double oven which would take care of all the cakes and turkeys she needed to cook for her big family.

We asked her if there was anything she wanted she didn't have, and her answer was what we expected from the Ann Campbell we had gotten to know in the past hours.

"No, not a thing. I have plenty to eat, I've got plenty of clothes to wear. I don't have a whole lot of money, but I have money to do the little things. My son is seeing to me being in a new house if the Lord lets me live. So I really don't know of anything; I just couldn't be any happier than I am right now."

Happy, yes, but was Ann ever lonely in spite of her big family? Had she ever considered remarriage? The answer was a firm "no".

"Not at all. I just felt like I could never find a man I could adjust to with eleven children. I felt like me and the children were two parts. I didn't think I could find a man to fit in with us. I had my family. I had all my babies. I wasn't planning to start raising another family, and I had companionship of all ages of people, so I didn't need anything else.

"I see so many young people living together without marriage, and I don't go for it at all. I just can't stand it. I think it's just a ridiculous thing. I guess I feel this way because my parents taught me to marry. If you find somebody you like well enough, marry. I think that's what held us stable.

"I think a good age to get married is around twenty-five. If people get married much younger than that, the wild edge will come out sometime or the other, and after they are married something will come along that turns them on, and they will go through that unsettled stage after they have other responsibilities.

"I think they should go to college and just kind of get themselves together, see a little bit of the world before getting married."

Ann had given us her views on marriage, families, race relationships, and rest homes. We asked how she was experiencing inflation. Was it a big problem for her?

Her answer was easy, like her other answers; she had thought the matter through, and she knew where she stood.

"I don't notice inflation much. I find it is possible to manage on a low income. If you're in the country you can raise a lot of your food, vegetables especially. I've even killed yearlings and put the meat in my deep freeze. I hardly ever buy any vegetables because we raise our peas; we put up peas and we put up corn. And that way we can live a normal life. A lot of times when the other staples go on sale you can save by shopping the sale way—that helps."

But what about doctor bills? "We've had a pretty healthy family, we never had too many doctor bills, and we've always been able to pay our debts. The doctor delivered my children, most of them. And, of course, my husband took care of a lot of things."

Life, inflation, and doctor bills, the world problems on the first page of the newspaper are not particular worries to Ann. She has an answer for them.

"I don't worry too much about it. I feel like everything is going to fall in place. The Lord is going to see to it. He is going to take care of us and so, I just really don't worry about the different things that are happening. When I think about the problems and the future, I feel most of all I would love to see my children, all children, be good kids and I'd like to see the dope and drugs cleared completely away.

"A long time ago I set a goal for my life, and that one goal was that, after being married and blessed with these children, I would raise my family and stick with them. I could have walked off and left my kids; but I wanted to take care of them and raise them the best that I knew how."

Nothing in life has been a big disappointment to Ann, she told us, and she believes it's because, in her words, "I haven't been an extravagant person who was just reaching out and expecting a lot. So that's the reason I suppose I haven't had much disappointment. Looking back on life, though, it has been rough, and then it's been good. But when I look back it's been a lot of fun."

Before we left we again studied Ann's smooth face reflecting back on memories of responsibilities discharged faithfully, even as she looks forward to a life in the spotlight of her son's career. I saw her little house which had been filled for over thirty years with the laughter and sadness of a vigorous family. I felt the stability through it all, and I couldn't resist saying, "Ann, you are a wise woman."

She answered as I knew she would, without emotion, untouched by anything so casual as a spoken compliment.

She said simply and courteously, "Thank you."

Dorothy Moore, a corporate wife, is representative of a large segment of American wives today, since she has spent much of her adult life alone with her children while her husband has been engrossed with business affairs. She has acquired skills and developed talents to add interest to her life.

8. Dorothy Moore

Enjoyable Days Through Her Skills

"I don't know that I could say I have paid a high price, either. I can only say that I have probably built a different life from the one I would have built if he had been at home with me."

Dorothy Moore's hands are her metaphor for life. Her hands sew, weld, paint, collect, garden, lay brick, polish stones, and upholster; and this is only a partial list of her activities.

Her home is a showcase of her many talents, and it is filled with pieces of driftwood sculpture, Mexican art, gems, sea shells, and a woodland of vigorous plants which spill over into a greenhouse of rare orchids and bromiliads.

But all these activities did not arise purely from a need for expression of artistic talent—they developed from a need to fill a loneliness which was created by what may be viewed as good or bad, commendable or blameworthy, enriching or depriving. The evaluation applied will depend entirely on the viewpoint of the observer, for Dorothy is a corporate wife, the wife of a financially successful husband who has excelled in his field because of his willingness to spend long hours and even weeks away from his home.

Dorothy is no anomaly in today's society. There are thousands of women who remain at home, rear a family, and fill their lives to the brim with interests while their husbands are away working. And perhaps Dorothy speaks for many of these women as she attempts to look back over a life and decide whether it has been good or bad, desirable or undesirable.

She says, "You ask me if it has been good or bad. I know my husband would say it's necessary, and I would say I don't know. He would not be where he is if he hadn't worked this way, so I wouldn't have gotten the benefits of what he has accomplished. I do know that he has never said that he has paid a high price for his success, and I think he has enjoyed it. I think that he would do it all over just like he did. I don't think he would change a thing. And I may be wrong, but I think he has thoroughly enjoyed everything he was doing.

"As for me, I don't know that I could say I paid a high price, either. I can only say that I have probably built a different life from the one I would have built if he had been at home with me.

"Given the circumstances I had, I took the way I wanted; I just got out of the house and did other things.

"I'm a loner anyway, and that's fortunate. I was a loner as a child on the ranch. I was not unhappy when I was out there by myself. Somebody else might say that I have paid a high price but I don't. We've lived parallel lives; we've gone together parallel. And our marriage only began to really work when I started living this way, when I started building my own life. I could not have stayed and been the little goodie, goodie wife keeping house and cooking meals, hoping he would find the time to come home to eat them. That life plan could not have worked for us."

The word parallel means "lying evenly in the same direction, but never meeting, however far extended." This definition was described well as Dorothy said, "I'm not hanging onto him. I'm not upset anymore when he's off because I now have my friends and my interests."

There are areas where the parallel structure varies, and that is on family vacation where scuba diving is the center of interest. This is an interest which crosses all lines and becomes a shared activity.

Books and newspaper columns point out daily that there are almost as many different kinds of marriages as there are marriages. Dorothy is quick to point out her conviction that marriages change because of the stages of growth of the marriage partners.

Dorothy can pinpoint such a change in her own life when she was in her thirties. She can't account for what brought the change about, but she does feel she has observed the same change in her friends at about the same age. She feels that she definitely took a different attitude toward home, children, everything. As a result she began to develop private interests. She began to read a lot of books on psychology and marriage, and she began to see the pieces fall into a different pattern.

She evalutates the change. "I think partially it was a change in the world in general, and I think too that what happened to me was probably there all the time; I just started to recognize it.

"I was beginning to ask, 'Is this all? Where am I going from here?' And I knew if I was going anywhere, I had to do it then. I couldn't wait until the children were grown and then decide I was going to do something. This period was a traumatic experience. I just realized that I had to build a complete life for myself, and I was forced to start that building process. That is when I turned to all the crafts and a career."

She thinks loneliness played a big part in her decision to get out and build her own life. "Here's the situation," she says. "Nobody in life, I don't care how well they like themselves, can live alone. I knew that before we moved from one city to another, which was when this all came to a head. My husband was gone three weeks and home one week. This went on month after month after month. It was very upsetting for the two children because Daddy would come, and he'd boss them around for a few days and then he would disappear. Then I'd have them all to myself for three weeks. It was an impossible situation. Perhaps that was when I was gearing up to do something different."

As it became apparent that Dorothy and her husband's lifestyles were in unalterable conflict, many people would have planned for divorce. Dorothy did not. We asked her why.

"We stayed together mainly for the kids, I think. Women still didn't have the rights they have now. I could have gotten a divorce and taught school the rest of my life. My husband would have married somebody else, started another family, and my children would not have had a father; they'd have had a stepmother. They wouldn't have had any sense of security. We stayed together for the same reason we stayed in one community all those years while they went to school. They were stable and they were settled, and we knew if we moved and put them in a new school, we'd have a lot of problems.

"I'm glad I did it the way I did because I think I did more or less what I wanted to do when I did it. I think I can do more or less what I want to do now, because I've got my freedom. Now that is the one thing my husband always gave me. If I'd been married to someone else, I would not have stayed, but I could always be free when I wanted to. I went to Mexico and studied for six weeks, and I'd go to Europe by myself. He doesn't ever hover over me; he's so busy with his work that he can forget he's got me, and I don't make ripples. This is something somebody else might not like, but for me it is fine.

"I think that probably then the only reason I would have left was just to show him that I could make it on my own and find somebody else who stayed at home with me. So what would I have done? I wouldn't have accomplished anything."

Dorothy left the home-mother role for further education and a teaching career which lasted for eight years.

She says earnestly, "There is something I think young women have to realize if they want to save their marriages. When you're left alone a great deal, you either get involved with going to college, or you get involved doing something for yourself, or you go to night clubs and bars, and you wind up in a bunch of places you're not supposed to be."

Dorothy began to look back into her past to see how she had handled earlier experiences before her teaching career and craft development. She had gone to work several times before;

she had been a teacher, a Social Security employee, and general financial worker, but these jobs were more to fill in a short interval of time during her husband's military service, or else they were responses to a feeling that she simply did not like to stay at home. They had not been real career investments. She had liked having her own money, and she had escaped the house. These were her early reasons for work before her decision to build a complete life.

In her childhood she could perhaps see her experiences of freedom and also of self-reliance building into a life pattern. She was born to a pioneering family in a log cabin in Blue Water, New Mexico, with a mid-wife officiating. Her father had driven a hundred horses to New Mexico without knowing much of either the climate or the mountain terrain, and the horses simply walked into the snow drifts and disappeared.

When she was six weeks old, her mother brought the new baby back to Texas on the train while her father followed and brought the few surviving horses.

They settled on a ranch, twenty-eight miles from the post office and sixty miles from the nearest movie. Dorothy adds philosophically, "And today the town still doesn't have but five hundred people in it, and still no movie." Her early life was spent moving from the ranch into town to attend school in the winter and back to the ranch for the summer.

She tells of her early lack of companionship. "I had no playmates, though I had brothers and sisters, all younger than I. If I played with someone I saddled my horse up, rode ten miles across the mountains, and visited a little girl and spent the night with her. Then the next morning I got up and rode the horse back home. Maybe a month later she'd ride over to see me and we'd play again. We were close to the Concho River, and after I got older, I'd walk down to the river and fish. I taught myself to swim with my mother sitting on the river bank scared to death, holding a stick so I could grab it if I thought I was going under."

There was a different type of "going under" which threatened even more than the undertow of the river—it was the pull of the Depression.

Dorothy remembered, "It was just getting over, and I think the Depression had a lot to do with the way I feel about life and everything. I was at an age where it did hit me hard. It hasn't affected my younger sisters; it was not a threat to them as it was just a few years earlier. During high school my mother would send me up to my grandmother's farm every summer for about six weeks, and I'd have to help cook for the crew that threshed the wheat. Then I'd come back home and work. We had very little during the Depression, which was really rough. We had food to eat because we were raising our own food, but we had no money.

"We did have a telephone, the kind that you cranked up. I remember that so well because of an incident that occurred. My grandfather built the line all the twenty-eight miles out to the ranch, and there's a law that says you have to let anybody tie onto your line if there's no other way that they can have a phone. Grandpaw wanted some rent from these different people and one man wouldn't pay his rent, so Grandpaw would go out there, climb up this pole, and cut his supplier off. And this man would go out, climb up the pole, and tie back on.

"This went on until finally they went to court. The case got so funny the judge had to clear the court because one of the prosecuting attorneys said, 'Mr. Evans, just about how many times did you climb up the pole and cut your neighbor off?' He said, 'Golly, I've climbed up that pole so many times it's plumb slick.' That was what ranch life was like then."

Dorothy made certain, firm decisions as a result of living on a ranch during the Depression. "It made me determined that I was going to college, and that I would not live on a ranch. I decided I would do something I felt I had some control over. When you're on a ranch and it doesn't rain, you have no control whatever. You're out of cattle feed; you're out of water; you have no way to manage your life. You sit there and wait

until it rains. I just couldn't sit there. And so when I went to
school that was my purpose in going—just to get somewhere I
wouldn't have to live on a ranch. I liked the country, but I
would never go there to make my living. You have some good
years and you have some bad years. It's just too 'iffy.' "

The word "alone" is certainly one of the key words in
Dorothy's life, but while she had been alone much of the time
during her childhood, she insisted that she was not unhappy.

She feels that one of the contributions the ranch made to her
life was the development of the ability to be solitary for periods
of time without being lonely. It is apparent that she filled her
solitary hours with activities just as she did later as an adult.

"I learned to catch bugs and snakes; I had all sorts of pets.
One summer I had two hoot owls until they kept Daddy up all
night with their hooting, and we turned them loose. I had a fox
and I had opossums and squirrels. I had a badger once and a
porcupine.

"I was aware of rocks, and although there weren't many
pretty ones to collect, I dragged in the available ones, dug up
cacti, and caught all of the animals I could make pets of."

There were the pets in the summer and school in the
winter—the unique situation of all the ranch families moving
into town near the school. Her mother was devoted to the
children getting an education, and Dorothy must have shared
some of her enthusiasm. She remembers that she was a good
student, that she skipped the second grade, and that she was
valedictorian of her seventh grade.

High school was fun with the river available for swimming,
parties at home, football, softball, and even tennis. High
school over, Dorothy left for college, still with her mother's
hearty encouragement. She majored in business and minored
in English, economics, and government for a most logical
reason: she felt that these fields would help her get a job as a
teacher, or as a secretary if she couldn't finish school.

"I never knew for sure whether I would have the money to
be back the next semester. It depended on whether or not it

rained. I took typing, shorthand, bookkeeping, and then it rained. I took all the courses and then just kept going. I was lucky and finished."

Dorothy doesn't feel she had a strong determination to succeed. Mostly, she says, she was having a good time. "I could have done much more if I'd had more determination. I did definitely have the goal to finish college, though."

She feels that she had a very bad inferiority complex at that time. She says, "In some ways I did feel that I was not as well-prepared as the kids coming out of the big schools. I could keep up with them, though, and I could make A's. Then I'd get off on a tangent, go to too many football games, have too many dates, and then drop down to B's. My inferiority feelings were not about my abilities but about me personally. I had a lot of kinks I had to iron out."

She feels that the "kinks" are tied to her background. "My grandmother and grandfather on my mother's side were German, and they were not sociable people. They lived out on the farm and did not mingle; they spoke German until World War I and stayed very much to themselves. My mother was that type of person, too. When you put that with living out in the country and not being around a lot of people it has an isolating effect on you. I never had to make friends so I didn't learn that social skill early. My friends were made for me before I was born. There was a little town nearby and I knew everybody; my parents knew everybody, so I never had to make a friend. They were always there.

"I'd never had any allowance; I'd never had any money. My father was very strict, and I'd always had to be in at a certain time and tell him exactly where I was going, and when I was coming back. He had a lot of funny, little quirks about how I was to dress. He wouldn't let me wear slacks. When I was just a little girl, I couldn't wear ankle socks—my socks had to be up to my knees. And I always had to keep my feet firmly on the floor—a bunch of stuff like that was impressed on me."

Commenting on the burdens of being the eldest child, she said, "I broke my daddy down and the later children had no problems. Those poor older ones indeed carry the load where parental silliness is concerned."

She recalls rebelling quietly by doing things her daddy didn't want her to do; however, she feels that her parents were basically satisfied with her performace during childhood.

Following college graduation Dorothy "left one frying pan and went into another." She left an all-girls' school and went to an all-boys' school to work on the campus.

This experience she remembers as her first total freedom. "I had somebody on me from the day I was born, and now I was free." The following year of freedom is still a good memory for her, but Dorothy doesn't feel that she would necessarily want to extend it, even if she could go back.

"I think it was a growing period," she says. "As soon as I had gotten in one stage, then I was ready to move on to another. I think it was a stage of development. I've always laughed and said I was just a slow learner when it came to social development, and of course social behavior was all boxed in by so many rules then.

"I'd been up at college four years, and I'd been dating guys in college, and I had the college rules to go by. And we had plenty of rules. The system was that the parents checked the rules they would allow for their children. My mother checked that I could go out of town and spend the night, but she didn't check that I could go to town and come back the same day. So when I'd go out, I'd go and spend the night. The reason she checked that going and spending the night was acceptable was that I could go with some of my roommates over a weekend, and it all came under that one rule of leaving the campus. She didn't want me running in and out, so I'd go and spend the night. There are so many unreasonable things in a child's life.

"World War II had started, and I was working on the campus. I was thinking about joining the Waves. Mother and daddy just had a fit. They thought I was going into prostitution, so that dampened some of my enthusiasm."

Shortly after this Dorothy met a young economics professor on the campus, and they decided to be married. The engaged couple did not go home because Dorothy felt there was a risk.

"My Daddy had a habit of making fun of every boy I'd ever dated, and I decided it was going to be my decision. We were working six days a week all the time, and I just called home and told them I was getting married."

Dorothy looked at her development since that time and says firmly, "If I could go back to do it over with my present awareness I would have joined the Waves. I would have been even more adventuresome than that!"

There had been another opportunity for adventure which Dorothy says she would have taken if she'd been able to experience the mental and emotional freedom she now has.

"If I hadn't been married after a year I would have gone on to Alaska to work, but I was talked out of that, too. I had my papers and everything ready to go up to Alaska and work. I was going to do that as soon as my husband shipped out overseas. But instead, that's when I stayed, came back home, and taught school in a little town."

Dorothy sees the reasons for her return to the little town as an expression of the times, and also as a result of the pattern of her upbringing.

"The pattern set up by my parents was that the woman did what the man wanted her to do, although my mother was very good at getting around it and bringing daddy around to doing whatever she wanted. It's a different world today; girls can do whatever they like and most husbands applaud. I only had a choice of maybe teaching school or being a secretary. I don't know what else you could have done at that time.

"If I could have joined the Waves it would have been different. I had this friend in the Navy. He begged me to join because he said with a degree I'd go in as an officer, and I wouldn't have to come up through the ranks. But there was something in my background that made me hesitate to do it. I just wasn't ready yet. That's exactly what it was. I just wasn't ready.

"Children now have a broader education socially. They see more of the world. I had never been out of my state until I went to college; in fact, I had never been more than two counties away. I guess my grandfather brought me to Austin once. So from West Texas to Austin was the farthest I had ever been. That limits you so, and it doesn't build horizons. You can't know what to do, and you don't have any counseling because your parents have never been anywhere. They'd never done anything but ranch, so they had no knowledge of what opportunity there was. It was just a matter of muddling my way through."

The feeling of the war years was apparent in Dorothy's explanation of why she had married at that particular time.

"I think I was following the herd; I felt it was time to get married. I had worked two-and-a-half years, and during the war there was a feeling that life is 'here today and gone tomorrow.' You'd meet somebody, they'd be drafted, and were off and gone. Then you'd never see them again. We would give parties for the guys going. It was war time. Nothing was stable, and nothing was planned. I don't think we planned anything.

"I think maybe both of us felt it was just time for marriage. I think there comes a time in everybody's life when they feel they are ready to get married. Then they're going to find somebody who feels the same way, and that's why the two get married. I think it's just a matter of two people in the same stage of development or the same place in life that happen to meet and get together, and it might happen with any one of several people.

"Marriage was an adjustment for me, and I think I realized there were other options at the time, although I couldn't deal with them. I had been interviewed to work in Washington for a man I knew. I had almost forgotten about that job, and I hadn't been married but about a week when I got a telegram asking me to come to Washington, D. C."

Dorothy looked back to the climate of her attitudes and the attitudes of her parents in the forties and she says realistically, "But I don't know that I would have gone, either, because I was not that adventuresome. I was always wanting to do these things, but then everybody was trying to keep me from it so it was almost impossible to fight the tide of family opinion."

Dorothy very early started satisfying the needs within her by turning to crafts and skills to fill her time. She gave us a partial list of her skills and accreditations acquired over the years.

The crafts and interests began in childhood. There were the pets, the collecting of rocks and plants, and then the field of expertise broadened. Where there was the possibility of competition she was a winner.

"In high school I won a trip on my sewing and I made my clothes. And then—I did play tennis in high school; I went to the district meet on that. I started raising tropical fish. All along I have been strong in gardening. I always come back to that. The other things I would do for awhile, and then I'd put them down, but gardening is always with me. I've collected minerals; some of them I've collected at mines, and some of them I just bought, and I joined the Gem and Mineral Society. I got certified for scuba diving about two years ago and I've learned to weld."

Welding is an interest she explains by saying, "We had all the equipment for welding in the garage, and I was familiar with some metal art pieces, so I just decided that we had all the equipment out there and nobody was using it. I just took some lessons and made a few pieces.

"I've done some oil painting. But I'm not getting enough fun out of that for the time it takes. I think I'll quit. I went back to the university and took some courses in basic design in art. I studied principles of design. I've taken some courses on interior decorating, and I had a Berlitz course in Spanish. I then went down to Mexico to study Spanish. I did that because we have talked about moving down to Mexico after retirement.

"I took a real estate course, and also a course in upholstery—and did a sofa. I made all the draperies for this house; I've done brick work and built patios. I built a fish pond with the boys' help."

She summed up her truly impressive list of skills by saying, "Anything that I want to do, I'll attempt. It may be crazy, but I'll try it. And if I have the physical strength, I think I can do it."

It was apparent that Dorothy felt no fear or hesitation in entering new skill areas. She believed she could do the work, regardless of how far it was from her previous experience. We commented on this, and she had a ready answer.

"It just wouldn't matter to me if I couldn't do it—I'd quit."

Dorothy reads widely, so much that she is getting off the magazines because they are repeating themselves. Reading is another of her activities which she can enjoy alone, and this ties in with some further observations about being a loner. Places are in general more satisfying to her than people. Yet, she has no feeling of anger against people. She feels that she genuinely detests no one, but she adds quickly, "People do not affect me so closely that I could really detest them. I mean, I'm not that close to people."

With characteristic modesty she says she hasn't contributed anything unique to the world.

"Anybody else could garden, keep a house—we all do that. I have reared two sons, but there are many fine sons in the world. So, you know, I don't really feel that there's anything outstanding. I really don't."

She sees herself as a generally happy person, in, as she says, "an introverted sort of way."

She sees the requirements for a good marriage as being shared interests and the willingness to experience a lot of give and take in all areas—work, home, children, everything.

Looking back, her two children have brought the greatest satisfaction to her life, and the biggest difficulties have come from trying to keep house and dealing with the schedule of routine tasks repeated over and over.

Dorothy feels she has built a freedom in activities for herself and that this gives her a good life. She was shaped by her early ranch years, her solitary mother, and her own tendency to be a loner. She affirms that she has taken all her given circumstances and shaped them into a whole.

As we left, Dorothy told us that she honestly felt her skills, all in all, equipped her to work with landscape architecture. We had the feeling that, considering her devotion to accomplishment, we might well return to find her credentials for this additional field hanging prominently beside her other certifications. Skills are her area; she had built her life around them. Where there has been loneliness, she has filled it with a new proficiency—and the proficiencies have built a contentment. Her mastery of her life has come through skills. To her it has been a mastery built on new interests and the joy of freedom to accomplish.

9. Evelyn Roberts

Oral Roberts's Wife, Alert to God's Miracles

"The person who has no problems and no needs feels no affinity for our ministry. Our supporters are the common people, just like us."

Oral Roberts University lies in the rolling hills in suburban Tulsa, Oklahoma. The buildings are all startlingly new, and the campus brochure announces that the "buildings and facilities have been designed and constructed as a part of the University's concern with excellence—a modern, upward-looking approach to a campus with down-to-earth principles and policies."

It is not hard for the visitor to accept this statement as she is guided from the brilliant blue-carpeted Christ's Chapel to a television-equipped resource center or a fireside lounge. All these are a part of the university which opened in 1965.

The Prayer Tower which centers the campus lifts a flame 200 feet into the air. It is architecturally designed to symbolize a twentieth-century cross with a "crown of thorns" around the observation deck. Also located on the observation deck is the Abundant Life Prayer Group where people are available twenty-four hours per day to handle telephone prayer requests. We dialed the number and received an immediate answer by a courteous voice which asked for the problem. We stated what we had on our minds, received a brief prayer about the specific issue, and hung up—all in the space of three minutes.

But as surely as the Prayer Tower centers the campus geographically, the presence of Oral and Evelyn Roberts center the campus emotionally and spiritually.

We met Evelyn in a business office which happened to be available at the time of our interview. The day was cold and snowy, and our hostess was dressed warmly in sweater and boots. Her welcome was easy, open, and friendly. Though her schedule is heavy, she has the knack of making her visitors feel that there is plenty of time. There is time for life on the ORU campus.

We had seen the neatly dressed students on the campus, each young man dressed in coat and tie with well-combed hair. We had been greeted and welcomed on the campus by passing students, we had eaten in the cafeteria where students stood back to let us go first in line, but we wanted to know what Evelyn Roberts saw as the unique features of the campus. Evelyn had a clear view of its uniqueness.

"We started this university because God said to my husband, 'Build me a university.' God wanted a university built on the Holy Spirit. Then we wanted to bring an education to the students that would be a well-rounded program for spirit, mind, and body—what we call the whole-man concept, not just an education for the mind. You can get that type of education from thousands of schools, and maybe more, in this country, but I don't know of anywhere you can actually get body, mind, and spirit education. What we have told our students is that this is a way of life, and within this way of life is an education. You don't come to ORU just to get an education—you come to ORU to learn this specific way of life.

Evelyn explained that a part of the ORU way of life was known as the "Seed Faith" concept. "This concept is involved with learning how to plant seeds of faith in your life by giving yourself to God first and then giving a part of your resources, a part of your money, a part of your time, a part of your talent. Whatever you do, whatever you have that you can give to God, you do it as a seed of faith which you plant. And when

Evelyn Roberts is the wife of evangelist and college president Oral Roberts. She is a part of the life of the campus and the dream for the "City of Faith," a complex of a sixty-story clinic, a thirty-story hospital, and a twenty-story research and continuing education facility which is rising south of the campus.

you plant a seed in the ground it grows. The way it grows depends on how it's nurtured, how it's taken care of, and then when it comes up it doesn't come up as one little seed—it's multiplied. You may plant two or three seeds, and you have a whole bunch of little plants that come up, so when that seed you're giving to God is multiplied, it not only helps the person you've given to, but it is multiplied back to you also.

"We're trying to teach people that God wants us to prosper; he wants us to prosper physically, he doesn't want people to be sick. He wants us to prosper mentally; he doesn't want people to have mental breakdowns. He wants us to prosper financially; he doesn't want people to be so poor that they can't pay their bills. There are many lopsided Christians who believe that the soul is alright, but it doesn't matter about the body, or they believe the body is alright, and it doesn't matter about the soul. What we try to teach our students is that God wants our bodies trim; he wants us to take exercise every day and take care of this body because he gave it to us; it's the only body we're ever going to have now. We built an Aerobics Center over here just specifically for the purpose of taking care of the body. Then we take care of our souls by doing devotions every day, by communicating with God, and by keeping our relationship with our fellow man right. You see, it's a well-rounded thing. And of course we believe in miracles. It's a miracle campus.

"Everthing that you see on this campus is a miracle because everybody said it couldn't be done. They told us there was no way in the world it could be built. Now they are saying there's no way in the world that the "City of Faith" over there will ever get built except by a miracle. That's the only way that ORU ever got built. So we believe in miracles—that's why our university is unique."

Evelyn's speech is direct and forthright. She seldom repeats a word or interjects a "you know" or "well." She is obviously a person who speaks often and is accustomed to covering a specific topic in a designated period of time.

She moved on to discuss the "City of Faith" which is rising

amid scaffolding and towering cranes across the street from the campus. It is a project as big or bigger than the University. We had read in the newspaper recently that the funds for the enormous project are already committed. A news report states that Evangelist Oral Roberts says that more than a million people have already sent him a total of 50 million dollars in pledges or contributions for construction of the complex.

The projected initial investment for the 1.9 million-square-feet complex is 100 million dollars and the completion date of Phase I is set for 1980.

We were eager to know who would be able to come to the hospital after it survives the many legal tangles surrounding its construction. Would the hospital be open to everyone? Evelyn spoke first of care for the partners, which is the title given to the people who contribute to the work of Oral Roberts.

"Of course, we're going to take care of the partners of our ministry first of all, because they have put money into it as well as their time, effort, and prayers."

She began to tell of the work which had enabled the hospital to arrive at its present stage of completion.

"When we were trying to get the Certificate of Need which is necessary before building a hospital, four hundred thousand partners sent letters requesting approval."

The brochure goes further to state that the main patient load is expected to be from among the more than 3.4 million families who consider themselves partners of the Oral Roberts ministry and the more that 25 million persons in America who identify themselves as Charismatic Christians. It tells further of the utilization of the facility to "provide clinical experiences for medical students and residents-in-training for the ORU School of Medicine."

Evelyn repeats that they are not building for local people but people from all over the United States, and the hope is that "just driving up they will feel God's Spirit and his power so strong, and hope will come into their hearts, and some of them will be healed before they ever get to the operating room or before they ever get into the hospital."

Oral Roberts states the same thought, tying it to the specific architectural feature of the construction. "As you drive up to this complex and see the Healing Hands and the stream representing the River of life, I know you'll want to get well. And wanting to get well is half of the battle of getting well."

The aim for the "City of Faith" is as clear in Evelyn's mind as the aims of the University which she had discussed earlier. "What we're trying to do in the "City of Faith" is to merge medicine and prayer. Now there are many many people who think they are so spiritual that they would never go to a doctor because it means you don't have any faith. There are other people who say they don't want any faith mentioned around them. They say, 'We have doctors; I don't need anybody to pray for me.' It really isn't either/or, if God wants to use prayer in order to heal me I'm perfectly willing. It's certainly more painless and cheaper than going to a doctor. But if the doctor has something that will cure me, then I want it. I want everything that God put here on this earth for me to use, and this is what we are trying to do here in the "City of Faith." We want to combine medicine and prayer and just see what God will do with both of them used together. Now that's a powerful force."

With the imagery which flows through the writings of Oral Roberts he had spoken elsewhere of "joining the healing streams of God."

Oral has made the treatment plan concrete by saying that the hospital will have a prayer partner in the "City of Faith" to pray for the patient when the doctor goes in to administer medication because "they belong together."

Earlier in our tour of the campus we had asked our guide, a ministerial graduate student, why the clinic was designed to be sixty stories and the hospital only thirty. He told us of their conviction that many people need prayer and encouragement more than they need extended hospital visits which are frequently traumatic to patients.

Legal problems continue to develop around the "City of Faith," but the three-towered complex does not hesitate in its majestic climb.

Mrs. Roberts spoke so easily of God's healing power and God's willingness to grant miracles to men, we tried to imagine how she had reconciled her faith with the tragic death of her daughter, Rebecca, who had died with her husband in a plane crash, leaving three children.

Evelyn spoke as any grieving mother would as she told us of the effect of the deaths on her life and understanding. "I'd been trying to counsel people and help them after their loved ones had died, and I thought I knew everything about it, but I didn't know anything. I didn't know that the first three days when people hear about the disaster they all come and your house is full of people. You're talking and you're crying, but you're in such a shock that you really don't know what has happened to you, but when everything is over and they all go home and you're absolutely alone, this is when it really gets to you."

She told of the fourth night after the crash when the grief was so intense she felt she could not bear it. As she talked with Oral, he assured her that with all their teaching to others, they had never before really needed the comfort about which they were teaching.

"We've known the power of God's Holy Spirit; we've seen him demonstrate his love and his communication through us, and now in our need we're going to pray in the Spirit and the Lord's going to help us."

Following his own constant teaching of Planting a Seed of Faith he told her that their recovery from grief would have to come through such action.

"We've got to go on television, just the two of us, and sit down and tell people about our grief. So many people have gone through the same thing, or worse, and they want to know whether we are real human beings and whether we hurt like they do. At first I said I couldn't do it. I just couldn't put my grief out for everybody to see, but Oral felt that we had to plant a seed of faith, or this grief was going to get us down.

"When I insisted that I couldn't do it, he said he would do it alone. I couldn't let him do it by himself, so about two days later he got the tape crew all together and told them that we wanted to tape half an hour, and we just wanted to go into a little studio and talk to people who are grieving. That was the hardest thing I have ever tried to do in my life; I just felt like I couldn't get through that half hour to talk about it all over, but I did get through it.

"I told how we went over and tried to comfort the grandchildren because that was my first concern. Here were three little children without a mother and father. I felt I couldn't bear it, but for the children's sakes I went. I told them about how Brenda was thirteen at the time, and she picked up a little plaque of ours that they had on the coffee table. It said, 'God is bigger than any problem you have.' She picked up that little plaque and kind of hugged it to her, and then set it down. I showed the people the plaque on television and I said, 'If you don't have a plaque in your home like this, maybe you need to be reminded when you're having problems that God is bigger than any problem you may have.' I realized that if Brenda, my little granddaughter, could realize that God was bigger than that problem, then we can tackle anything. When I got through I was drained. I was washed out, but I felt like we had a victory because I felt that we had planted a seed of faith in the lives of other people.

"Thousands and thousands wrote us that they were grieving. I found out that people lost daughters, lost sons, lost husbands on the very day we lost our daughter, and one woman came and told me she lost both sons, her only two children, in one year, both of them with heart attacks. I thought of how I had felt I was the only one who had pain and grief. So it helped all of us to share the hurt. They could relate to us in our hurt, and after we did the taping I felt a great release. I just felt like I had planted this seed, and something good was going to come out of it. The Holy Spirit comforted me to a point I've never been able to explain to anybody, although of course I've never gotten to a place where I don't hurt for Rebecca because I do miss her terribly."

Evelyn continued to think of her grief as she told of an experience of lying on a mat taking exercise. She spoke of feeling so lonely lying there until after awhile she spoke, "Jesus, I don't know how you could have let this happen. You took her away from those three little children who desperately need her, and I just said, 'You're not a mother, you don't even understand. How could you understand what I feel in my heart losing my child?' Then just as if He spoke to me I heard the words, 'Oh yes, I understand and my mother understands. Remember? She stood and watched me die.'

"Of course I had to ask for forgiveness because it is easy to forget that Jesus went through death, his mother went through it, and so many have gone through it."

Evelyn spoke of practical steps she took to help her grief. Music, especially hymns, could lift her out of the doldrums. "Songs just do something to me," so she began to utilize them.

She spoke of a period of exhaustion which came about six weeks after Rebecca's death. Through reading the Bible she understood that the joy was gone from her life, and she felt that this was the reason her strength also was gone. She turned to music. As she shared the music, joy came to her again. She saw this return through music as a return to life itself because, "When you lose a loved one, you have a tendency to withdraw from the world. You think about the dead and forget the ones who are living. So my music brought me back to the living." She turned to the positive results of the death as she said, "I've done a lot of grieving; I've been able to help a lot of others in their grief. The children are growing and adjusting in such a way that I never would have believed, so there are so many good things that have happened; the Lord is bringing good out of bad."

It was apparent that Evelyn Roberts had known difficulties in her life in addition to the loss of her daughter. She recalled a childhood in which her parents were divorced when she was four years old. Her mother remarried, and soon her new family became interested in spiritual matters including Christian schools for the children. She told of traveling from one community to another in pursuit of a Christian school. "We had a wagon in those days, and my mother and dad would put a quilt on straw for us children to lie on in the back of the wagon, and we would strike out and go to any meeting where we could find the Lord." With rich conviciton she adds, "I wouldn't take anything in the world for the Bible background that I got."

She speaks of reading the Bible through and of yearning to be a missionary, but at eighteen when she had finished high school, passed an examination for a teaching certificate, and taught school for a year, she met Oral Roberts who was also eighteen. And her life changed.

Her grandmother was a strong force in her life, encouraging her to study and prepare herself to teach. Evelyn recalls her grandmother's refusal to permit her to use any slang and her urging toward education.

"Now Evelyn you are going to set your goals high. You are going to get the best education that anybody ever had; you're not going to stop till you get right up there and get your degree. Then you're going to marry somebody that's going to make something out of himself."

It was this same grandmother who cried out, "Oh, Evelyn, I had such high hopes for you. Now they're all gone," when Evelyn announced her plans to marry a young preacher named Oral Roberts.

For her the meeting with Oral was a case of love at first sight. They met at a church camp where they were each playing a musical instrument in the church services. Oral also remembered that she sang a solo and that in his words, "It was the worst song I had ever heard."

He sent her a gift of a book he had written for her twenty-first birthday with a request that they begin a correspondence.

They corresponded from April to September, and then Oral came to see the girl he could scarely recall having seen at camp.

His mother came along with him because, as she said, "If you're that interested in going 850 miles to see a girl, there's got to be something going on so you're not going by yourself."

In the crowded weekend Evelyn and Oral escaped in his car and there he proposed to her.

She sees their meeting, their life together, the ORU campus, and the "City of Faith" all as parts of a miracle. She even looks back to the naming of her husband Oral as a strangly prophetic and miraculous experience. She told the story of the naming of the new baby who was later to become her husband.

"When he was born, a cousin of his helped his mother with his birth since she was something of a midwife. His mother said to her, 'Since this is my last baby and you helped me with all of them, I'm going to let you name him.' The cousin bathed Oral, took him in, and sat in the rocker. As she was rocking him she said aloud, 'I will name him Granville Oral, and we will call him Oral.' So he was named Granville Oral.

"Years later, after we were married, Oral went out to interview her one day and he said, 'Minnie, I want to ask you a question. Where did you get that name? How did you happen to name me Oral? Did you know what the word means?' She said, 'No, I don't know what it means.' He told her that it means 'spoken word,' and he also told her that for the first fifteen years of his life he couldn't speak because he stuttered so badly." The name seems to her highly prophetic of the time he would speak to millions in spite of his early problem.

Evelyn speaks of the threads of divine guidance and intervention she and Oral have experienced together, of his decision to join the Methodist Church, of his long years of teaching and conducting healing services.

"The word 'healing' has had a devastating effect on people. I don't know why. Perhaps because for many years the churches didn't preach healing, and people thought that you were some kind of a heretic if you preached healing, and my husband did preach it. He preached that God wants people to be well.

"There was a lot of controversy in those days because they called Oral a faith healer, although he never did ascribe that to himself. He never did like the term; he hated it in fact because he said that nobody heals but God, and he was only God's instrument. But people called him everything under the sun in those days. They just didn't understand healing, and he was a pioneer in bringing healing to people. There is quite a change now. The Episcopal churches lay hands on the sick; Lutheran churches lay hands on the sick; Catholic people lay hands on the sick. Oh yes, there's such a change now. People may call you a faith healer, but it doesn't have the same connotation it used to have, but twenty-five years ago it wasn't like that. I resented that part of it; it had a bad effect on our older two children. They had to go through an awful lot because their daddy was talked about, and it was in the papers that he was a fraud because of his healing. In those days there were even stories that he wore a wire up his arm to shock those he touched when he prayed for people and, oh, they circulated such foolish things."

Healing and speaking in tongues or speaking in the prayer language are the two concepts which are often associated with the Oral Roberts charismatic ministry. Evelyn told us of the development of the terms charismatic and prayer language. Evelyn admits there are wide differences of opinion on this subject among Christians.

Speaking of these experiences she said, "When I was growing up we called it the baptism of the Holy Spirit. This was all I ever heard it called; I never heard the word charismatic until we first began hearing about the new charismatic movement. I asked what it was because I didn't know, and I was told that it's people who are filled with the Spirit, and I said, 'So that's new?

I've known it for fifty years.' Maybe it gave people a feeling of not being in the category of the Pentecostals to give it a new name.

"What happens is that the Holy Spirit enters and with him comes an inner knowledge of a prayer language, and when we release this prayer language—speak it and put it to use—it releases our spirits inside. I guess my husband started the term 'prayer language' simply because about eight years ago he started teaching a class on this experience, and it was called 'the Holy Spirit in the Now.' The Lord began dealing with him to preach the baptism of the Holy Spirit. A year or two before that he had begun preaching it in the crusade before we stopped having the crusades. The Lord started dealing with his heart. For a long time he just couldn't preach on it because he didn't feel that anybody understood what it was. He said he began praying for the Lord to give him a term that people could relate to, and he began preaching about communicating in the Spirit, and then he introduced the term prayer language."

According to Evelyn she received the experience when she was twelve years old, and went on to say that the language can be interpreted sometimes by the speaker and sometimes by a hearer.

With a practical and thoughtful note in her voice Evelyn added, "The experience is under the control of your will, and your emotions should be under control. It's only when people get hysterical that it turns people off.

"There's nothing wrong with the experience of the Holy Spirit, but the people who have the experience sometimes just don't know how to handle it, but this often happens in other areas of life too. How do we know how to handle such a precious gift as this gift? Sometimes we don't handle it right."

It is apparent that each part of the teaching and the total ministry is real to Evelyn Roberts, so we asked her about the

3.4 million families who consider themselves partners in the ministry. Who are they? She instantly pinpointed the supporters.

"They are the common everyday people with problems and needs. The person who has no problems and no needs feels no affinity for our ministry. We do have a few people who come here that don't have any problems or needs, and they love the ministry and are partners with us. For the most part, though, that little woman out there who's been left a widow and can hardly make a living for her four or five children finds that this ministry has met a need in her life. It has shown her that God wants to meet her needs. She may send us one dollar a month as a seed of faith, but because of that she gets her needs met. People that she had no idea would ever come to her door give her money; people bring her food; somebody will pay her rent anonymously.

"Our supporters are the common people, just like us." She added with a laugh, "Oral says he has only a few millionarie friends, but he prays for every one he has. It takes a lot of little gifts to make something go, and when people give, you not only have the money, you have the people, and it takes people to put something across."

Before we left we asked what the slogan "Expect a Miracle," which is so much a part of the Oral Roberts ministry, meant to her.

"It means that every day of my life I'm alert to the blessings that God has in store for me. So I'm just expecting them; I'm alert to what God has for me. That's the way I look at it."

Evelyn Roberts' sincerity and dedication to hers and Oral's ministry is a vibrant and real force. As we left to go out into the snowy Tulsa evening we found that we too were newly aware of the world about us. It did, in fact, seem to be a world of miracles.

10. Mary McFadden

Zest Through Creativity and Hard Work

"If someone wants to be beautiful they do become so. Even if their form was originally ugly, if they have that desire, they do become beautiful, specifically the older they get. This is something I think is really important because I've seen it happen so often. If they don't care about beauty, they remain ugly; if they want beauty, they become beautiful."

There are so many small, unique worlds within the world. Mary McFadden's world is made up of color, design, float, drape, pleat, and quilt, and over it all hovers the aura of creativity and beauty.

Her designs are for the upper one percent of the market, for those women who have both the time, money, and interest to study the most subtle nuances of fabric and style. But a conversation with designer Mary McFadden reveals that there is much business sense and self-discipline involved in her world which expresses itself as fantasy and inspired beauty.

We took a taxi to a New York address on West 35th Street in the Garment District where trucks filled with racks of plastic-draped garments honk and fight for parking at the curb. This is the location of Mary McFadden, Inc.'s, sample room and showroom.

We were met by willowy Shirley McGill who showed us into a ten-thousand-square-foot area where decorative cascades, jewelry displays, pieces of African sculpture, and brilliant splashes of clothing design dominated the overpowering space. A few clothing racks held silks and quilted jackets which were interspersed with the designer's most important trademark, the Marii-pleated robes.

By the time Mary arrived we were somewhat dizzy from the impact of a sea of soft green and rich orange designs mounted under glass about the walls. We were reveling in the hand-forged brass jewelry, some pieces studded with semi precious stones, and charmed by the intricate knotting of macrame hangings.

This was the world Mary in six years had shaped with creative imagination, primitively sketched drawings, sewing machines, and choreographed showings of original collections.

Mary is a self-portrait of her own world of fashion from her sleek black hair to her strikingly combined rose skirt and braid-trimmed jacket with the easily recognized McFadden hip-draped belt. We did not feel surprised to learn that she had been listed on the International Best Dressed List since 1963, and has been elected to the Hall of Fame. Nor were we surprised to know that in 1977 she was listed at the top of the Best Dressed Professional Women's List.

Mary McFadden, Inc., had been formed in 1976, and we marveled that she could have gained such recognition so quickly. She assured us that in design this is the way it develops. She said, "If you look at the history of couture houses you will note that after almost the first collection, they were established. If you aren't established by selling within a million dollars the first year around, you might as well walk out of the field. This is the pattern."

But how had she made her unique mark in a fiercely competitive world where the men and women vie twice each year for the position of direction pointers for not only the look of American women but women throughout the world?

We sat at a long table as Mary quietly massaged its surface with hands which seemed to demand the feel of rich texture even as she talked and analyzed her rise in a sphere which she sees as a combination of show business, art, fantasy, and competitive business.

All her jobs, including design and journalism, she told us, she "fell into backward." Hers had not been an experience of

Mary McFadden is listed by Women's Wear Daily *as among the top twelve designers in the world. She is a two-time winner of the Coty Award, as well as being the recipient of numerous other prestigious awards. Clothing, jewelry, upholstery-weight fabrics, wall hangings, wallpaper, and perfume are among her areas of design and manufacture.*

carefully set goals painstakingly achieved. "My whole life has been a surprise. I didn't expect to do anything I've done. When I entered the fashion field I had no long-term goals at all."

Mary speaks of surprises and falling into opportunities for success, but this is no easy success which she is thinking of. Hers is a philosophy of success by the individual who is willing to stand exposed at the point of challenge. "I myself have never really been aware of my potential as a human being until I have stood on the firing line. Maybe this is true of other women; maybe they can never know their potential without that challenge of being confronted. I had my firing line first in journalism, then business, and now design."

The rewards of standing on the fashion firing line have been impressive. Mary won the Coty award, not once but twice, in 1976 and 1978, as well as the Roscoe, the Rex Award, and the Legendary Women Citation from Birmingham—Southern College. She was also awarded the Governor's Award from the state of Pennsylvania, and many others. One of her most recent honors has been a doctorate from the Rhode Island School of Design.

But Mary's experience with cloth and design did not come suddenly or without work. In fact she started designing her own clothes when she was thirteen years old, simply because she couldn't wear the boxy shapes and heavy fabrics in fashion then. Since Mary now holds her weight to ninety-five pounds on a very small-boned frame it is not hard to see that the soft-dressing look which became associated with her was the design which would be most flattering to her own build. "I created a soft-cut that would elongate the figure."

She had neither a degree in the field of design nor any business education when she entered the field, and her early years seem far away from collections and shows.

Her childhood years were spent on a cotton plantation in Memphis, Tennessee, until in her teens she moved, with her two brothers and mother, to Westbury, Long Island.

She graduated from Foxcroft School and continued her

studies at the Traphagan School of Design in New York and Ecole Lubec in France. She later majored in sociology at Columbia University with additional courses at the New School for Social Research.

After a period as director of public relations for Christian Dior, there followed years in Johannesburg, South Africa, where she became editor of *Vogue South Africa,* as well as a columnist reporting on the political and social life of that area and other African republics. In Rhodesia she founded a sculpture workshop, Vukutu, for African artists. The Shona serpentine sculptures from this workshop have been shown in Paris at the Musee Rodin, Musee de l'Art Moderne, and The Museum of Modern Art in New York.

In 1970 she returned to New York and became special projects editor for *Vogue,* followed by the forming of her own firm in 1976.

But the door to the fashion world opened with three tunic dresses which were bias cut on China silk. She wore the tunics to *Vogue* magazine, and they decided to run them on the cover as a new direction. The designs were bought by Henri Bendel, and he encouraged her to manufacture. These first samples were made in a tiny east eighties basement in the August heat on one sewing machine, and this was the important beginning of the so-called "soft dressing" which took hold across America in 1972 and 1973.

Then there was the quilted jacket which was much in vogue in America and in Europe shortly after that. This jacket appears and reappears in a wide variety of designs wherever the Mary McFadden label is known.

The talent for design appeared early with Mary, but its development did not follow an easy path.

"I think the talent was with me very early, and then it disappeared. I think I was technically a very fine draftsman up until the age of ten or eleven, and then for some reason I didn't like my art teacher, so I just took no more art classes. But then I started collecting art. From the age of seventeen on I had a tremendous knowledge of contemporary art and sculpture, musicology, and museums. I was also married to a museum director. I suppose that helped, and I also chose art as a hobby, something that appealed to me. But I never took any further courses in school. My grandmother gave me a bunch of jewels. I sold them and started my own collection."

The courage to launch out into new fields had run through Mary McFadden's remarks, but there was little evidence of personal ego in her references to her awards, her references to designing for the most wealthy women in the world, her design expertise, or collection of art. She commented on this.

"Well, to talk about the ego problem, I guess most people think because there's a huge amount of publicity, and it becomes so distorted, that designers are thought of like movie stars. I think that's something different because we're on the firing line twice a year with major collections. Any designer can get a four-star showing one year and be panned the next. That's a tough thing to live with, and there's no way to get full of yourself in that kind of a life-style.

"Criticism is tough to accept, of course. But to have a collection panned, that would be really difficult. I've never had it happen, but I can always see it happening, you know. There's no question about it. I have a tremendous fear before showing each collection because a lot of things can go wrong; for example, the model can fall down and break the rhythm of the show. These shows are done in front of two thousand people so just the number of people and the excitement of those people make you quite nervous. There is no question about it—there is a lot of tension."

Mary has no specific woman or prototype of a woman in mind as she designs. "I try to make something so simple and classical that it will fit from a size eight to a size twenty, and the concept of it is color-oriented, so I think I can make a woman more beautiful than she might be otherwise. That's what I start to do."

Mary wants each woman to be more beautiful, but when we

suggested that a woman in one of her exclusive designs might become a Mary McFadden, rather than her own original self, we received a vehement denial.

"No, I don't agree with that at all. I think a woman should have enough character that she can wear the clothes and use them in an imaginative way—for instance, she can interchange the coloration. Like what I have on today. You look at these clothes rarely because I think the human character, the human personality is so much stronger than a mere design."

Does a fashion designer accumulate a large wardrobe for herself, we wondered. Or is the designer a bit like the shoemaker's children who are legendary for being without shoes. Yes, in a way, we found the designer is like that shoemaker's children, yet with a basic difference—the designer is always wearing bits and pieces from beautiful leftovers.

"I don't have any clothes at home whatsoever. I take whatever is discarded each season and have about four or five discards at home I've thrown together. This [she pointed to a piece of her striking outfit] is a discard. This is a sample; this is a return from a store. This is something that wasn't used. But I put them together. Anyone can do this by studying style, but it is second nature to me now. Any woman can add her own ideas,but also she might consider that the designer has worked out the idea for the ensemble in her mind hundreds of times, and there's no way to improve on it. So I think that buying a total design is the easiest thing to do. Putting one together requires some time. So why not buy it ready to go?"

Mary's jewelry is designed on its own rather than as a part of a complete design. It is a separate element. But she says, "Funnily enough, whatever I make always becomes a part of something else. It all works together."

One of the unique characteristics of a Mary McFadden creation is that she inspires and develops the fabrics as well as the cut. The total concept is hers.

She says that this is different from other designers. It is a "totally vertical operation." Her total design begins "when I conceive a collection. For example, the last collection was called the Ice Cream Palace Collection. I conceived it in about ten parts. The main aspect of that collection was the color."

Even the words describing this collection are pieces of creative imagery. "Fauve images and cut-outs are the melody of the hand-painted gauzes. Blocks of jumbled up mosaics create new engineered color washes, and chiffon pajamas are handpainted in Portuguese tiles."

The new collection is called "Nomads," and the imagination is even more unique here. "I conceived this as an imaginary time and place, basically a primitive time when people wandered the desert and were wrapped in heavy fibers and patchwork quilted with large stitches. It was a fantasy period, and the people probably never appeared at all the way I imagine them to have been dressed. So I think that this collection is a fantasy like all the collections are a fantasy, but the shapes are classical. There is no answer to how many Oriental and Middle Eastern cultures are represented in it."

The time schedule in preparing a show is awesome to consider. "We actually make the collection in five weeks, but I think about the collection for six months. We make one hundred five specific costumes. Some may have three or four integral parts. There will be twenty-five best-sellers from the collection, and the volume on each collection will be about one million dollars.

"There are many steps of preparation. I put the ideas on paper in a primitive manner, and the next step is selecting all the parts and working on all these fibers. You have to think of one hundred five garments and multiply that by three. There are a lot of fibers in each collection, and besides that maybe twenty-five jewels. Then there are the shoes, the hats, and the accessories.

"To make the collection we have about twelve women at sewing machines, and then later it is contracted out to make samples. About eighty-three stores carry our designs now; they're in all the top stores across the country."

While Mary talked of totally original collections and fabrics designed for a specific jacket or robe, we asked about style for the less wealthy. What did she feel was the significance of style to the American middle-class woman?

She thought long and seriously about our question. "We find in the industry that when we make lines for one hundred dollars, style isn't important. It's a very simple, classical cut just two years behind styles that we're showing in our main line. It's so pared down and so simple that it is a classic, and it will go on forever. But a woman in modest circumstances can definitely have style. I think that's the most interesting part of it all. An African who just has cloth and knows how to wrap that cloth has a certain sense of style. There is, I think, almost a God-given and innate sense of elegance of how to put something on your body that will compliment the body. It reveals a knowledge of how you can make your body elegant and beautiful. That's something which seems to be inborn, and you sometimes see someone with whom nothing goes wrong in their gestures or adornments. Notice the dancers who have that, but they study it. It's very rare to meet someone in whom you notice not one awkward movement. They're born like that.

"There is style in every economic level. In our own line or in the couture area, which one percent of America can afford to buy or have the leisure time with which to be associated, we find women who are interested in being individuals with their groups and having something on that other people will notice. They aren't interested in fading into the crowd. It seems to be the difference between class structures. It's the way they've been brought up. The wealthy have been brought up so they talk about clothes because they have the leisure time to do it. They have the money to do it. The working girl doesn't have that kind of time—therefore it's not that important to her.

"It happens in decadent societies: for example in the Italy of the 60s, women had so much time to spend on themselves they could be involved in themselves. They could be more frivolous about themselves. They could go have their hair done and things like that.

"Now in that one percent they do go to the beauty parlor at least twice a week, and they do have face-lifts; they do have their hair dyed; they do study every new cosmetic change. They have the chance to read all these magazines, and they're involved in the communication of all these new products. It is the same all over the country. In Texas or wherever I am I find the one per cent again, pretty much the same. There seems to be sort of an internationality about these types of women. They are tremendously rich, of course. I don't see much difference from one country to another.

"Clothes may not make a woman, but they certainly project her. They project a woman's sense of personality, whether it be conservative, extroverted, or artistic. From that point of view I'd say you couldn't say that clothes 'make a woman,' but you could say they emphasize what a woman is—they define what is already there."

We had heard comments and read articles saying that women had become more independent in their style. We had heard it repeated that women would no longer be told what to wear, but Mary did not agree with us.

"In style, while it is highly controversial, I have always maintained that most Americans follow herds. They're like sheep. They go to each fad when it comes. There are very few people who can escape this. For instance, the skirt is now slit and shortened, and there are really searing articles in the papers to show how out of fashion specific people are with longer skirts. And those people are going to shorten their skirts just because they are going to be tremendously upset about being different from others.

"I personally think that the slit skirt is beautiful and we have it in the collection. Also we shortened the skirts to two inches below the knee for the spring/summer scene. I thought the collection was much more beautiful that way."

Mary points out that there is always much movement in

styles. "The soft line was almost out the last six months because of the hugh influence that came from Italy in the military, big-shoulder looks, the so-called futurist looks or retro looks. It's been coined both ways. This is something that's always fluctuating backwards and forwards between soft and structured, tailored looks. Most designers have a tailor on their line, and most designers fluctuate collections between soft and tailored."

We wondered how a busy woman such as Mary found time for the many details of cosmetics and grooming of which she had spoken. How could she participate in the time-consuming beauty activities?

"If you want to find time for things, you can find time. That's of course a premise. And the next premise is that you have to be organized.

"I organize my time for exercise and make-up very carefully. As you see, I have a rather complicated make-up on. It's like applying a painting really. There are many colorations and shadings of the face, as you can see, but it's so subtle you don't notice it. Anyway, it takes about five minutes to achieve it the way I want it to look. The clothes take no time, obviously, at all. And I do exercises. We have several machines at home. We have a bicycle, we have a rowing machine, and I do push-ups. I do about twenty pushups, and I do about ten minutes of exercises a day. I haven't had any time to play sports recently because of the incredible amount of time I have to spend in my business. Since I weigh about ninety-five pounds this means that I have to be highly disciplined to keep that weight. So I just don't overeat. I know calories by heart, and I know instantly how much I can have at each meal. I mean I know how to pace the day's food intake so I won't gain weight. I'm highly disciplined about food.

"My mother is also a highly disciplined person. She's a concert pianist, and she spends about six hours a day playing the piano. She's done that most of her life, and I think she's a very artistic woman. Maybe she hasn't had the chance for education that I've had, or perhaps she never chose to give it to herself, but in music she's very well-trained."

But even with all the self-discipline and organization Mary says emphatically that if she were starting today she would not go into the field of fashion. "It is too time-consuming; it is a very difficult business because so much product is required.

"I work at it all the time in my head. Actually I come down to the factory at 9:00-9:30 and leave at 5:00, but that doesn't mean I stop working. I do both the design and the business, and that makes for a very busy life.

"I have a total of sixty people on my payroll for home and factory. At home, I have a live-in woman, Maria, who is chief bottle washer. She can do anything. She can cook, she's a clothes expert, and I have somebody who assists her. Then when we give a party we bring in help.

"We're giving a dinner tonight for eight, and we're going to give one every week for the next month and a half. I have a lunch here nearly every day. I think it's very nice to have a lunch here as opposed to going out which is difficult because of the location that I'm in. It would take me half an hour to get to my destination, and this way I can come right downstairs from my workroom and have lunch with whomever I have here that day. We have some wonderful food here, or we go out to Macy's delicatessen and pick up chicken salad or cheesecakes, or whatever, and we can make a very nice lunch for any number of people."

Although Mary had told us of her busy schedule and assured us that she wouldn't go into the time-consuming design world if she were starting now, we pressured her for information about how a young person could best enter the field.

"I think they should go to Fashions Through Technology, Traphagan, or Parsons here in New York. And they should study there to see if the field appeals to them first. It might not necessarily appeal to them, but it might lead them in to another direction. I would suggest not even going to college. Instead, I would suggest starting right away working in an 'etalier. If she knows that she wants to be a designer early, she has such a running head start, and in this business, where technical ability is so important, she can always learn later how to broaden herself. Of course, I know this is not what's being done, but this is how I did things and of course, everyone I employ has also had this type of training. They knew what they wanted to do. They had an innate sense of elegance, a sense of design, and then because they had that talent they could develop themselves, and they didn't waste any time. Fiddling around with all different types of courses sometimes doesn't really help.

"Today young women's options are infinite. I think the most important thing is to decide right away, by the time you're seventeen what you are going to do. If you're going to be a lawyer then go on into that. And then, of course, with that kind of training or some training as an accountant, it's infinite what kind of bureaucracy you can get into and work yourself up. In the case that you produce products, which I find very few women are trained for since it's an area that doesn't exist in schools, you really analyze it or you train in a sense. If you can produce any product, just think what that can mean in terms of creating anything you want! If you want to be a psychiatrist or a doctor, human experience internationally, just by virtue of communications today, creates all possibilities. It's just unbelievable."

Mary had spoken of her interests and work, especially in journalism and fashion. As we asked about her other interests we found that a door had been opened into many other worlds.

She is interested in the theatre, dance, travel, collecting art, musicology, museums, jewelry—and, of course, the stones and fiber, ceramics and glass which fall into the category of art. She is heavily into interior design, architecture, and architectural interior design, as well as the study of furniture which she is working on right now. She is also interested in the history of rugs and rug designs.

Her approach to an interest is browse in her own library first.

With characteristic creative imagination she immediately added, as she thought of the field of rugs, "But that's not how I would design rugs. I'm happy I have that backlog on rugs because I would do something totally different than had been done before. But you have to know, of course, your market before you make a product.

"If you want a select market a product can be extremely radical. The more radical it is, the better it will sell in a select market. If you want to reach a mass market you have to give them the most classical, easily comprehended product that can possibly be produced."

Someone had described Mary's designs to us by saying they were paintings in motion and we asked her if this seemed a fair description of her work.

"I think it's fair, but I would also hope that they wouldn't take this as meaning that they are too fragile to be worn and worn hard. They are a part of the workaday life; they are designed to be worn."

A beautiful display of a Mary McFadden new perfume, in a uniquely designed bottle at the center of the room, had captured and held our attention. As we asked Mary how long she planned to stay in the design field, she gestured toward the perfume and said, "I have a perfume contract which reads that I have to be in design as long as I'm alive. This new perfume will be on the market by Mother's Day."

We had talked of the workings and philosophy of beauty, which is the core of design, so we felt it would be good to know Mary's definition of beauty in fashion.

"The woman's inside coming outward, and if someone wants to be beautiful they do become so. Even if their form was originally ugly, if they have that desire they do become beautiful, specifically the older they get. This is something I think is really important because I've seen it happen so often. If they don't care about beauty, they remain ugly; if they want beauty, they become beautiful."

The creative expert had spoken: she said that beauty is possible for all who seek it. Perhaps this is the seed of genius, to realize that all is possible and only the search is needed.

Joanne King Herring is honorary consul of Pakistan in Houston. In this position she is developing world-wide markets for the handwork of that country's women. She is an international hostess who numbers kings as her guests, and she has been a television talk show hostess for over twelve years.

11. Joanne King Herring

Guests and Glamour in Her Life

"The most worthwhile thing I've ever done is trying to help women in these terribly poverty-stricken countries to make some money . . . developing markets for their work so they can feed their families without the cultural shock of going into a factory."

We scanned the photographs in Joanne Herring's living room as we waited for her to come down for our interview. They included everything from bathing beauty poses to close-ups of our hostess with King Hussein of Jordan.

It was an impressive array, but no more impressive than Joanne herself who showed up with purse and fur in hand, prepared to move on to her next appointment after we had finished.

Everything about her spoke of fashion, but she was ready to share the details of glamour and excitement which surround her life. She was also eager to talk about the price one pays for each triumph.

"You have to decide how much you're willing to pay for it because it does have a price, and for every triumph there is a tragedy—usually."

We began to talk of the project, the challenge of international scope which is taking so much of her time. "The most worthwhile thing I've ever done is trying to help women in these terribly poverty-stricken countries to make some money . . . developing markets for them so they can feed their families without the cultural shock of going into a factory.

"This is so rewarding, and I've worked twelve to fourteen

hours a day on it. When I was in Pakistan I literally stayed up all night and worked all day the next day many times because I didn't have much time when I was there. This has to come out of my time, but I got to thinking about what we could do. It seems to me the world is crumbling around us, and that our way of life is threatened. So what we have to do is help other countries realize that free enterprise works for them and for the poor. And we need to remind ourselves what a privilege it is to live in a country where it really doesn't matter what your background is. You can achieve anything.

"We have to ask, 'How do we help these very poor people?' So I chose a country, Pakistan, where I am the consul. When I started my work for Pakistan, I began to love it, and I fell in love with the president as a person, you know, as a man dedicated to his country. So I tried to think of a way to help.

"Emilio Pucci, who makes the most beautiful clothes in the world and is a good friend of ours, told us that he did not make anything in factories. So I thought, *Oh, wouldn't this be wonderful if we could help these people who sew on that thin, thin silk to market their work with designers such as he?* Some of these people live in villages, without even roads, not even a bicycle; they are totally isolated, but they do the most exquisite work. So I thought, *What if we could provide a market and teach them not to make hand crafts, but to make things that will have a sale value in the Western world, things that England, France, and the United States no longer make, because they can't afford labor costs?*

"I thought of the things that all of us would love to have, in the price range that we could pay. I tried to plan for the money to go directly to the workers so they would immediately see the benefits of living in a free society. Hopefully—we could start by paying just one worker in each village. Let the other people use her as a role model, and then put all the workers on a sliding scale, so whoever does the best work and gets it in on time, gets more money than the other people. This way the people have an understandable incentive to work and to work well. This is very important because quality control is such a big problem in the third world.

"Pakistan is such a new country they've never had opportunity to develop markets because they've been so busy just surviving.

"When we started our work, the women couldn't believe it because they had simply not been recognized. The government officials would say, 'Why haven't these people come to us?' I would find someone doing beautiful work in snakeskin, and the leaders simply were not aware of their work. The women need to learn about demand and markets, and they need many things such as hardware for purses, but they have such potential."

Our mouths began to water at the display of beautiful cloth, embroidery, and even guest books Joanne had assembled for us to look at. She held up one treasure after another as she talked.

"This is gauze; it has a tiny little bit of pink woven in there. But then we make jackets and they become an heirloom, something you would keep in your family forever. Look at this. It is all embroidered by hand, all in real silver or gold. I want to make this as a wedding dress for my children, and look at the back of this piece of embroidery! Of course, this is weeks of work. This is a copy of my grandmother's lace blouse, but you see that would sell in the American market.

"The duty is 30 percent when these are imported, but I'm trying to convince the State Department that this is handwork. This is handicraft just as much as anything done by hand. Just because it's gorgeous, why should it carry more duty than a basket? But, see, I'm mounting a campaign to get all this done."

Joanne spoke very seriously of her motivation in her work as she said, "I feel very strongly that God puts us in places because we are supposed to serve. So I felt, what can I do for Pakistan? And I thought, *Well, I know the chairman of the board of so many companies.* So by golly, I don't have to start at the bottom and work up to help them; I'm going to start at the top and work down.

"And I remember when we first decided to have the show of Pakistan products everyone laughed at it. They said this is impossible. Nobody can take a whole country, particularly a country where they don't even wear dresses, and teach them how to make dresses and change the whole economy of the country. They said, 'You're crazy.' There's only one person who didn't say I was crazy, and that was the president of Pakistan. And whenever I think about that, tears come to my eyes.

"This man said, 'If you can do this for my people, there is nothing I won't help you do.' And so I called on him when I ran into trouble over and over again, mostly with men telling me, 'Oh, now that's a wonderful idea. It's so fine and kind of you to do this, but it's really impossible.' Or some said, 'You must go very slowly because they're really not ready for this sort of thing.' So then if I got in real trouble, and I couldn't get over that mountain, I'd call the president and he'd call me back in five minutes. Busy as he is he'd say, 'What do you need?' And I would get something done.

"When we had the first show here, we sold out, absolutely everything. And we had it in the middle of the summer which is usually a poor time. That was our experiment. We're much better now because a lot of the things that were there, I wouldn't have chosen to be there, but a lot of the things were extremely good."

Joanne remarks that some of the aspects of her work remind her of the work in Appalachia. These women too were helped individually to do their own native crafts and market them. "In order to succeed with this type situation there must be someone who is knowledgeable and who knows other people who can actually put products on the market. There must be a person who's the leader and who looks at the whole picture. I thought my years in television had taught me a lot about fashion, about what people wanted. I also had contacts everywhere, so I went to the chairmen of the board of the major companies. At first I got reactions such as 'the poor had better help themselves,' but later I got call-backs and even a letter from one chairman of the board who said, 'Joanne, if you believe that strongly, I will send you my buyers.'

"Now this is a wonderful thing because ordinarily you pay for the buyer's expenses, but he paid for them, sent them all down here. They came, and they got very excited about the products. They later wrote me letters asking how I was going to sell. I said, 'I don't know. I don't know anything about the retail merchandising end of it, but I'm learning.' They said they would help and they went back, and they must have spent three weeks putting together a formula of how to make it work.

"Now we are going to have a display center in Houston which I think will be really important because this is a big convention city. Nobody's going to order something from Karachi, so we've got to have the wholesale/retail business here. I say here because I can oversee it. Nobody's going to care about it but me, and since I don't work for money—I work for love—I will continue to give them as much as I can, though it will have to be actually, physically run by somebody else. We will have facilities for every organization that wants to come out and have a meeting there, and all the conventions will have parties out there. They'll have to pay for their parties, but it's going to be in my house where I formerly lived, which is very beautiful and big enough to hold about eight hundred people when it's opened up. So I guess that was one of the reasons I held onto this house. Behind it we have space for warehouses, and no selling will be done in the house, but behind it customers can go out and buy whatever they see.

"So, we're going to have a catalog, but people will not order from Karachi—they will order from Houston so they feel secure about it. We hope we'll have a big retail business because we're going to have a fashion show which is really unique in the world. We have every top American designer and a lot of Europeans now designing for us. So in our collection of about 120 dresses, we have the most beautiful collection of fashion you ever saw in your life.

"Also we'll give lectures on rugs. We'll show how they're made, and we'll talk about them as investments. Eighty percent of all Oriental rugs are made in Pakistan, so that industry is already highly developed.

"It all has to come a little at a time, but the organization is beginning to come together. They may have 100 women in a group and when the work is finished, they give half the money immediately to the women; the other half goes to educate the children and to provide medical care. This breaks the cycle of poverty because the children get an education. If they are capable of being a truck driver or a telephone operator, they get that training. If they are capable of being a doctor or dentist, they get that education. But they are no longer the little village boys that are barefoot, and they realize what can be done in the world. So what I wanted was not one or two of these organizations, but thousands, and it's possible! Getting the organizations has been very difficult, but we have vowed to get them. And again, God had a hand in this. I know he did. None of this could have been possible without him. You can work very hard on something and be very dedicated and progress can be about like a visit to the carnival in the house of mirrors. But we keep going ahead, and everything we try seems to work. So I know that God is involved.

"It is all so worthwhile, and when you see a woman's eyes light up with the thought that she can get a machine that costs $200, this breaks my heart. Two hundred dollars is not that much money, yet it can change her whole life."

In addition and frequently related to her work as honorary consul to Pakistan, Joanne is also an international hostess. We asked her about hostessing after commenting on her unbelievably busy schedule. She granted that it was busy and then quoted the elder of her two sons as saying,

"Mother, I used to worry about you, but then I don't worry about you anymore; you like living in a hurricane."

Joanne laughed and expanded on the idea, "I think there are some personalities that like to have an active life, and I think I am one of them. I like designing these things. I like going through magazines and thinking, *Ah! How can we do this or that?*"

"The world of hostessing is its own kind of a hurricane," Joanne assured us. "A party is so much work and it's so expensive. Whatever you do, you must plan. Actually I've been doing parties all my life because at my grandmother's I was always setting the table or doing something. It's ridiculous to think that you just snap your fingers or you hire somebody and they do it. That's not the way it is. You do it!

"The main thing you have to think of is how to make people have a good time. It doesn't make any difference how beautiful the house is or how marvelous the food, though the food should be good. Food should be one of your prime concerns; I don't feel hostesses think enough about the food. If you only have one dish, make it good. I would rather have one very simple dish, boiled beef with marvelous horseradish sauce, than all kinds of crusty things that are not so good. I would rather go to somebody's house and have the same dish over and over because you don't go any one place that often. Make one dish your specialty, but make it sensational.

"Of course, people make a party. And the way they are seated is terribly important. If you put somebody where you have two really sensational people on either side of them, they're desperate to know who to talk to. Now that means they have to give some to each side, but you'll still have a real good table and people will feel pleased about where they are.

"I like moving people after every course, and I try to have at least five courses, so I can move people all the way around. And then everybody gets to sit by the guest of honor; everybody feels important, and the adrenalin starts flowing, so they give a whole lot to each person while they're there because they're there a short time.

"I buy things around the world and mix them all up for table decorations, and they don't have to be expensive. You learn to walk into a market and find something that could be attractive on a table. Realizing that flowers cost a fortune, you can buy a lot of things you can use over and over again. For instance, I saw these butterflies that were mobiles, and I got a long table full of them. I can bring them out over and over again, and put them on mirrored tiles, and they're beautiful. By the time I bought the whole table it was no more than the flowers would have cost me for one night. Those big Mexican flowers that you can buy make a marvelous centerpiece. And then you put them away. Then I had little boxes made out of mirrors, and you can put whatever you like with them. My husband has a jade collection. That doesn't come out very often, but when it does it is special."

We asked Joanne how much of the food was prepared at her home and found that before the entertainment schedule got so heavy it was all done at home. "Once I even had 800, and we made everything." But she added, "I didn't want to do that again."

"I like entertaining; for me it's fun, and I know the formula because I grew up with it. That part isn't hard for me. What is the most fun to me is to think up new things to do. And you see, I've tried new ideas with heads of state where everybody was really shocked. They said, 'Well, but you don't do that.' I said, 'That's all the more reason you do it.' These people go to parties where everything's so stuffy and they're supposed to play a role. They sit by people they probably already know—or don't want to know. And what they would really like to do is have one night where they can relax and have a good time."

We suggested that Joanne would make a good first lady with her entertainment skills but immediately she said, "Oh, I would shock the country so."

She told of her party for King Hussein. She had invited "every beautiful woman I knew from all over the country. There's nothing more decorative than attractive people. They were all princesses and countesses from lovely families, and they were all good conversationalists. So everybody had a delightful time, and it was not the sort of party they were expecting.

"I always think about the guests. Now what haven't they done? What would be amusing for them? What helps them to mingle? Then once you make your house as pretty as possible, you just have to have interesting people, then see that they move around and aren't stuck in little groups—and you have a good party. Then I believe in artists and writers as guests if they talk well. I'm not all that big on having cultural people unless they have something to give. Everybody must be willing to give something, and then you have a good mix and a good evening."

We remembered Joanne's words to us as we had come in. She had said that everything has a price. She had told us of her victories, but we wondered about the tragedies and the cost.

"Everything has a price. I have felt always that I have had a kind of charmed life. Everything good happened to me, but everything bad also happened to me. One of the worst things in my life—and I love telling people about this because I think it's very important—is that I was a learning disabled child. I read backwards. Now they are finding out that there are many ways a child is affected by this. I had a terrible time in elementary school. I really didn't have any friends. Nobody wanted to play with me at recess, and I wasn't attractive in any way. And by the time I was in about the fourth grade I was not just the tallest girl in the class—I was the tallest child. And I was slow, and I had very bad teeth. I wore braces for eight years, and I want you to know, though, that one day my life changed.

"What my parents did was very clever. They had both been extremely outstanding in high school and college, and my father had been an All-American football player, the man most likely to succeed, and the most popular man on campus. My mother had been a beauty, and here they had this ugly duckling, and they just didn't want to have one—so they started having everybody over to my house all the time so I would feel comfortable.

Then my teeth got alright, I rolled up my hair, and I wasn't the tallest person anymore. And I became the most popular girl in school, which was a marvelous miracle in my life. But what happened was all that gave me confidence which helped me to overcome the learning disability. And later on I was in the National Honor Society and on the dean's list in college. When I made the National Honor Society, my mother cried. I thought, *Now what is she crying about? This is no big deal.* But you see, it was really a big deal to her, since a learning disability, especially then, was very serious because there was almost no way to reach those children. They are finding ways now, but in so many cases the children are terribly damaged by the time they get out of school, because they're made to feel inadequate. So I think when I did find myself, I wanted to do things well.

"Perhaps, as a result of this experience, I am sort of a perfectionist in a lot of ways, mainly because I learned that if you work longer and harder than anybody else, that's talent. I also learned that no matter how much talent you have, if you don't work, you won't get anywhere. And so if you'll just give it the best you've got, then you'll almost always succeed.

My mother says, "Do the best you can—that's all the angels can do." And that makes me feel very good.

"The learning disability was only my first trauma. At twenty-one I was told I was going to die after I had been ill for eighteen months. I was in the most incredible pain; I have never experienced anything like it. They used to give me doses of morphine, but the pain went on and on. Finally they found out that I had a tumor in my spinal column, and I was in the hospital waiting for the operation.

"One of the nuns came in and said, 'You know, I think that

you should be prepared for this.' She said that no one had ever gotten up and walked from this operation. Many people have said how terrible it was to tell me, but it was the grandest thing that ever happened to me in my life. It gave me a chance to prepare myself. I was young and thought I had my life in front of me, but I thought, *I don't mind dying because I really have had the most wonderful life.* I had the most marvelous parents and the grandest teenage life. School was a real pleasure for me, as far as getting along with people. I had won everything college had to offer and had every honor in high school. Everything had come to me so if I died, that would be alright. But living as an invalid? I couldn't see living that way.

"It took me a long time and a lot of soul-searching to be able to turn that over to God. And when I said, 'Not my will, but thine,' I went into the operating room for four hours, and I was a medical miracle. Later on, I skied, I rode horses; I did everything. I was completely reborn, you see, from this. So then I said, 'I really am going to give my life to God and follow in the path that he wants me to.'

"I had married very young, and I had this wonderful house that was such a lot of fun. And for somebody twenty-two years old to have such a house was a wonderful thing except it taught me a lot—it had a terrible price. It had marble terraces on the front and marble terraces on the back and every acorn stained it. The help situation was awful, and I had children, and it got very complicated. We had a lot of parties, and it was fun. Princess Grace came and it was a time of excitement, but it was not an easy period. I worked with so many major events.

"At that time the Consular Ball had been an abysmal failure for thirteen years, and finally it got to the point that nobody would come. So the Chamber of Commerce and the Port Commission came and they said, 'Please, can't you do something to make this ball a success?' I decided the best way to do something like that was to make people think it was hard to get invited. So we put out this publicity that you could come only by invitation, and then I got top Houstonians to host a table, so that sold out the ball. Well, people were so funny. They left town if they weren't invited. So it just shows how psychology plays a part.

"Suddenly this ball that had been a complete bust was the big ball in Houston. The funny thing was, I was trying to get some people from Washington to come. Well, we invited every ambassador, and the ambassadors just laughed at us. Finally we ended up with the widow of a Vanderbilt and the stepson of an ambassador. But the ball was a huge success and everybody had a great time. Finally the ball got to be such a success that the consular corps started giving balls to thank Houston for it. So I was so glad that that worked out."

Joanne was back to her thought of the necessary price. "But all during this period here I was. I had little children, had this enormous house, a very wealthy husband who didn't really have to work and who wanted to travel. And what did his wife do? She went to work every day at the television station at a job on which he lost money. But I loved my audience, and those were very lovely years. But then I had this child who had terrible asthma and almost died four times. He had pneumonia and during this period I was chairing balls. Honestly it almost killed me. Many times I went to work, after having been up all night with a child, and yet it made a very close relationship between him and me. I had just decided that I was going to fight for this child's life and that, by golly, nothing was going to stop me from keeping this child alive.

"I could be in one part of the house and I could hear him cough at the other end of the house. But then after I remarried, that hurt him very badly and this was another price, you see."

Joanne's first marriage had taken place when she was very young. She remembers it as a happy marriage in many ways, but she thinks of its end as "one of those tragedies that happen to a lot of people in marrying young. We grew apart, and we just really saw everything differently. And that is very hard in a marriage because if the little things are sacrifices to make, then when you have to make big sacrifices it's too much. Everything just becomes too much so it's too big a burden, and there's not enough joy.

"I think that's one thing about marriage, you have to have this common bond of the things you truly have an interest in. Then when it comes time to do the things you don't like, you don't mind it. But if everything is a sacrifice, that's no fun. But divorce is a terrible trauma to go through. I don't think that has ever been talked about enough. I think no matter how amicable the divorce is, it is as close to hell as anybody can get because your children are involved, your parents are in-volved—mine was the first divorce my family had ever had, so it was a terrible thing for them."

Joanne remarried, and she has experienced many of the problems which confront a second marriage, but she sees the experience as something to be understood and worked out with patience.

"I found out one thing about second marriages. That is that all the children were so sweet and they all wanted us to get married. But when we got married, suddenly the territorial im-perative was there, and it was very difficult for all of them. They wanted us to be happy and they wanted to be happy, and they didn't quite know how to put it altogether. And if I could just tell every woman who marries again one thing, I would say 'give it time.' We all want to rush in and embrace these children and love them and have them love us, and that's not possible. You don't even love a puppy over night.

"Remarriage is another trauma, but it is a lovely trauma in certain respects, but when there are children involved—and you love them and want everything good for them—it can be difficult. Remarriage of parents very often happens in the children's teenage years when it's very hard to reach them, since they are so involved with their own pain, the pain of growing up and finding out who they are.

"We all come from different life-styles, and we have such different personalities. I was raised in a family that yelled and screamed and laughed and loved and kissed and hugged. I always kind of cherished that. But if you were raised in a different atmosphere—where there's just as much love and joy, but it isn't quite so freely expressed—then you don't quite understand somebody who's the other way, and often they think you are being insincere. Now we have a good time together, and I'm deeply grateful for that. But there's no magic wand to wave over any situation. Life is all one mountain, and then a valley, and a mountain, and a valley. My father always told me that when things are going well, and you're at the top of the ladder, look for a soft place to fall, because you are going to fall. I have been on the ladder, and I have fallen off."

With the busy ups and downs of the ladder in the past, does Joanne have specific plans for the future? "I haven't been able to catch up with the present yet. Oh, I've thought about my future a lot, but I don't know whether I think about my future realistically or not, but I always thought I would like to work with children. I always felt like maybe someday that would be a role I would be expected to play, because I really love children a lot, and I worry about battered children. This has been one of the things I have thought about much of the time. So, I always wondered if I were alone maybe I wouldn't try to do something in that area, perhaps with a home.

"Then I dream of being a beachcomber or something really uncomplicated, and I would like to uncomplicate my life. I don't quite know how, but I would like to have more leisure. I have this place upstairs which is sort of a loft where you can look outside and see the clouds. I had visions of lying there and listening to classical music. It's been five years and I've never done it."

Joanne enjoys vacations, but these are not totally un-complicated.

"We took three weeks and went to Nassau with our children, and that was wonderful. But we like people, and we have a good time together, and on our trips it's very rare when we don't have a dinner or party. But sometimes we don't, and then this is a great privilege. Then in Houston, we don't go out. We hardly ever go out in Houston.

"I do try to have some time to myself though. I love to read. And sometimes I get to a point where I get mad and stamp my feet, and I won't do anything, and that's when I pick up a book and I do what I want to. I say, 'I'm going to do today what I want to do.' That doesn't happen very often, but it's good for me when it does. And then I can go back and pick up the threads because if you take on a responsibility you can't just cast it aside. You have to do it, but then we all owe something to ourselves.

"I love to jog. You see, I do that and I'm all by myself. As an only child I have needed to be by myself sometimes and my life is very public, even in the house. Everybody wants in the room all the time. Kids—everybody. So when I'm by myself alone, it's just a joy."

Joanne remembers one of the happiest times of her life as when her first baby was born.

"They told me I would never have a child, and so this was something else God gave me. They said, 'Oh, it's impossible, you will never ever have one.' My doctor was very fond of me so he said, 'Joanne, I want to help you adopt one.' I decided that was the answer, but my husband wouldn't let me adopt one. So I said, 'Alright we'll put this in the hands of God,' and we had our first son!'

"Then I decided I wanted another child, and I went back to the doctor. He said, 'Joanne, that was a miracle, and you are not going to have another child—get it out of your head.' And so he offered to find another one. But this wouldn't work either. Then I decided if I had had one, I'd pray again. And I never will forget it—I was taking a dancing class, I was leaping, and doing all that stuff. I had an appointment to go to a fertility clinic. I went to the clinic, and they told me they wished they could take credit for it, but I was two months pregnant. And so along came my second child, and I feel that I have had almost every experience that a woman can have.

"I'd been told that I couldn't have a child. I'd been told I was going to die. I had a terrible time in school. I was very unattractive. I have had a divorce. I have had his and her children. I've had a career, you know, and so I've really had an awful lot of experiences that people dread. Yet I've had every happiness that could be heaped on anybody, too.

"You know, I think it's so wonderful to believe that you have a purpose in life, and when that purpose is fulfilled, you go home. I'm not in the least afraid of death, having faced it. I know that death is not the tragedy. The tragedy is for those that are left behind. I don't want to be left behind; I want to go first."

Joanne left her home, walking out the door behind us and heading for a luncheon. We marveled at her verve, her dedication to the things she felt were important, and perhaps most of all, her utter determination to achieve the beautiful things she dreams of. There is no hesitation in her approach. She is rushing toward those things she knows she wants to do. She is confident that she has the talent to do them since, as she says, "If you work longer and harder than anybody else, that's talent."

12. Marjorie McCorquodale, Ph.D.

Explorer of Life and Thought

"Although some people don't think so, life is really very long. And if you don't prepare for it by developing a love of literature, art, music, and ideas in general, it can be a real bore."

We heard Dr. Marjorie McCorquodale speak before a club group on the eve of her retirement from teaching. The feeling she conveyed was of an explorer launching out on an uncharted path, surrounded by fascinating views never before glimpsed.

She felt that for a lifetime she had stored away in her mind ideas and self-investigated concepts and that now, with more time at her disposal, she could begin to look into these ideas more thoroughly.

We met her again two years later in her book-filled apartment. We discovered that she had indeed pursued her thoughts and yet, as any scholar, felt that she was only beginning to think through so much of the information and new research which was available to her.

She spoke of her years of teaching, but more specifically of her personal concept of teaching.

"I always felt that I had a very special bond with my students. In the first place we were engaged in a mutual exploration of ideas and meaning and a search for significance. We were explorers together. It was as if I too were a student, and we were together exploring the material. It was never my feeling that I knew everything. I never wrote out my lectures and read them.

185

I always talked directly from my material, and I always reread the work freshly every single time I taught. That means every novel, every short story—I reread each one before I taught it. And I never taught it the same way twice, because I always found something new and vitally exciting that seemed to be really pertinent to our lives at that moment.

"And, of course, there are fundamental things that one teaches about literature always: how to analyze and how to look at every aspect. And I always used the phenomenological method of analysis or approach to material. I would say this is the most penetrating, and also the most creative way, of looking at anything, because it consists, in the first place, of putting out of one's mind everything that one has heard about—whatever it is, whether it's a painting, or an article, or a novel, or a short story. It is a complete setting aside of everything that one has ever been told or has read about it. And you know some very famous works are so encrusted with the opinions of others that this is not an easy thing to do. But if you don't do that, you never can find your own perspective.

"And so, investigation was my method. Consequently, I was always learning too, and I think that's why I enjoyed teaching so much. I never thought of myself as a teacher; it's that we together were looking at this work to see what we could find out that was significant for us."

The word "explorer" works in and out of Marjorie's conversation. As she had approached her teaching as an explorer, she also approached her retirement as an explorer. She was offered several opportunities which she mentioned by brushing her hand aside. "Those were all too much like the things I had done before. I didn't want to repeat experiences in my retirement."

But then an entirely new experience opened before her. She with a colleague was offered the position of tutor to the Princess of Saudi Arabia. This was a new world to explore.

One of her first realizations as she entered her new field was

Dr. Marjorie McCorquodale, a member of Mensa, is a scholar and a thinker. She has been a university professor, a tutor of a Saudi Arabian princess, a writer, and a continuing student of life and thought. She views retirement from teaching as an open door into leisure for further research and thought.

how much more advanced women are in the United States than in the Middle East. She says, "It was not so much teaching the Princess as in meeting whole families that the overall position of women was apparent." She told of a specific incident which stayed in her mind.

"We were invited to tea by the wife of a man in an outstanding position. We were taken into their garden. When we walked through we saw a whole group of men in the walled and paved courtyard as we were going into the garden, but we did not join them. We were led by the children, and all the women and the young children were gathered there in the garden. We saw some of the parts of the house and a place in the back where they kept various kinds of animals. But you see we were kept separate, away from the men of the household even at a party. We were shown the goats, the chickens and the birds in cages much as small children would be entertained here."

The Princess however lived a different life. "The Princess had traveled so much she could not be thought of as a characteristic female even of the upper class. Now that did not mean she was bookish or intellectually so terribly far ahead, although she had gone to school until she was twelve years old. She had gone to a very special school for the members of the royal family and a few of their relatives. After that she had been tutored by a woman, a Ph.D. in chemistry, who then became her companion. This companion had done a great deal of work in mathematics, and she tutored the Princess in mathematics and sciences for the last years of her high school experience, because the Princess could no longer go to school with the other boys and girls. That was simply the way it was."

Marjorie described the Princess as extremely bright, and she applauded the Princess' special interest in psychology which the Princess saw as a way of understanding the people around her, the people of other nations, and other experiences. As a result of their interest in psychology, in discussions of literature the two examined the psychological factors of the characters and their motivation.

A moving story emerged showing one reason for the emphasis on education for the Princess. Her grandmother, immediately after the Princess was born, had stated emphatically that her granddaughter must have an education and that she must learn to read and write. Marjorie said, "I didn't understand the poignancy of this until months later when we were out in the desert. We were sitting on beautiful carpets in a tent which was opened to the east to get the breeze, and all of us were sitting, leaning against cushions. I drew a little sketch of the tent and some goats that were foraging on the shrubbery outside, and then I passed around the piece of paper I'd sketched on for everyone to sign, and someone else had to sign for the grandmother. She was a very wise woman, wise enough to know that everyone in the modern world needs to read and write."

We asked if Marjorie could see anything positive about the restricted lives of the Saudi women. How did it look from their viewpoint?

"If one thinks that the life of a child without any responsibility, except for the immediate family relationships, is an ideal life, it might seem to be so. The mothers have complete control over their children, including the boys, until they are fourteen or sixteen, and the mother remains an immense influence in the family. They have the extended family system so they always have a group; they always have their cousins, and so on, thus they escape loneliness. They always marry cousins, so this is an interlocking situation in which they may never get outside their family group during their whole lives. They may never even meet anybody who is outside the family group. It's much like being kept ten years old for life. Like children, they are given pets to play with. They are given little animals to raise, and they are never asked to deal seriously with any problem outside of relationships within that group."

Marjorie saw this as a viable life only for that person who had not become aware of the outside world. She adds that now this would include only the very poor since radio and television are increasingly present to inform all people of what is available elsewhere.

"It is no longer possible to be isolated. Anybody who has the stirrings of intellect, the stirrings of curiosity, and who learns to read is bound to experience frustration. And the thing that is increasing the frustration is that there is now a big program to teach everyone to read."

Changes are coming, and in fact are already in evidence because the government is building tremendous universities and high schools as well, and these will destroy the isolation of their lives.

Marjorie told of a meeting of some four hundred women which she had attended where Marianne Alireza, author of *At the Drop of a Veil,* spoke of the differences she found in living as an American in California and in Saudia Arabia and how it affected her. Marjorie said, "It was a talk that would appeal to the intelligence of women anywhere."

This transition to intellectual activities is an indication of many changes. The presence of women from all countries in Saudi Arabia has brought about a part of this change.

"Foreign women there and the women of the upper classes do indeed go to school. In fact, all the girls are now going to school for a certain time. And even mature women who have been married and divorced, or lost their husbands by death and who have grown children, are now going in the primary schools and high schools. I knew one of these who was a relative of the Princess, and she was studying English. She was also studying the history of the planet. Now you can see what change this is going to make in the thinking which until now has been quite restricted with respect to, for example, science. And all the children are getting this education, so you see the effect on the next generation."

Although change may be imminent there are vast differences of thought and life-style between Saudi Arabian and American ideas of home life. Many of the differences are created by the marriage laws which Marjorie had observed in action.

"A father can have four wives at a time, although I didn't know any who had that many. But it would not be unusual for there to be ten children in the family. It might be that a wife had been divorced, but the children would stay with the father unless he chose to loan them to the wife for a short time. The law says the father gets the children."

The Arabian experience added an entire new facet to Marjorie's understanding. "There were so many new things about the life there," she observes, "and they were extremely meaningful to me, even though quite different from anything I had known. I could relate to them well. I could relate their worship to my own feelings of reverence, and there's nothing like the desert to give you a feeling of reverence. The vastness, the starry sky at night, and the moon high up create a moving experience. I really felt no conflict; I have no problems about being critical of the religious practices of others or feeling alienated because of them. These things seem to me like beautiful expressions of the reverence for being that we all feel and sometimes don't express so well."

The desert experience could be accurately identified as a totally new direction of interest, rather than as an activity of retirement. It was truly a new door into life. And there were also other doors.

Marjorie did some writing for NASA on the topic of the moon in literature. This writing grew out of earlier research and intellectual discussion. It was a culmination of many conversations with scholars from other fields of interest. Again, we were into a concept which is of great significance to Marjorie, the concept of the unity of all learning and the unity of all ideas.

She told of the beginning of her investigation during university days. "At that time the faculty had a club in which we all ate. That means it was a gathering place, and the university was smaller then, and practically all the faculty members at some hour or other would meet there for lunch. There were individual tables so that meant you came in personal contact with all the faculty members from all departments, which was a great advantage. As I more and more talked to people in sciences, and with the beginning of NASA and all the space development, I became increasingly interested in what changes in our literature, in our attitude, and in the way we express ourselves would develop as a result of the space program. I wondered what changes in the way we use our language and our metaphors would develop. I felt much about space science and astronomy was so technical that I decided to start a discussion group to meet on Thursdays at noon in the faculty club.

"We met and I told them I would like to see us discuss, over a period of weeks, how the scientist could now describe the universe to us in terms so that writers, students of literature, and poets could find new metaphors for our fiction and our poetry. We can't talk about the moon in June now that man has walked on the moon. We can't even talk about the moon and green cheese. We've got to have some totally new metaphors. And in order for poets to make new metaphors, a poet must have a description of the way the scientist sees the universe. So I asked each of them in his discipline to tell us how he described the universe in language we can understand. So this is what we did."

The very fruitful conversation resulted in Marjorie's receiving an invitation from the National Science Foundation to submit an application to study at Oak Ridge and participate in a month-long discussion with scientists, and a few people from the arts, on science and contemporary social problems. She remembers the conference as being attended by some of the outstanding scholars of the age, as well as Ralph Nader who served as recorder. Marjorie was the only person from the South and the only woman participant.

Marjorie's lack of fear in plunging into new areas of thought, she feels, goes back to her great independence in childhood. Although she was born in Chicago she recalls the early move to El Paso with her soon-to-be-divorced mother. She recalls being cared for by a maid who had lived all over the world and worked for army people. The woman was very precise about all the small things and utterly unaware of general life development.

Marjorie says, "I had to eat on a plate with a napkin in the dining room. I couldn't go out carrying a sandwich in my hand. But aside from that I was literally my own boss all the time. In other words, I cannot remember a single instance where anybody ever told me I ought to do my homework, or that I ought to study, or that I ought to do anything. I just lived in an absolutely free environment, except that I had to have good manners about my eating habits.

"In the summertime, I went to bed when I was sleepy, and I got up in time for school, but nobody ever told me to. I just got up because I loved school. And so, consequently, I think I've not been very amenable to external discipline most of my life, and I see that as both a fault and a strength. I think I've missed a lot of things and I've been far too independent in many ways; on the other hand, I have followed my interests because of this."

A further evidence of her early encouragement to independence, as well as total self-reliance, is seen in the story of her first automobile. She laughs with delight as she says, "I really think this is the biggest joke. It was my birthday so my mother walked in and said 'Marjorie, with your heavy schedule at work and in school, I can't see any way you can operate if you don't have an automobile. So, I bought you an automobile for your birthday. It's out in front. Here are the keys. Go out and drive it! That's the truth. Literally the truth. I'd never driven a car before. I had ridden with a family friend of ours who often took my mother and me out, and with an awfully nice man who had a Buick convertible. The only time I ever touched a car was when he had to go somewhere to a hospital to see someone, and he left me parked in this convertible out in front on the side of a hill. We were parked by the edge of a cliff, and all of a sudden I realized this car was slowly rolling backwards toward the edge. That was the first time I had really ever thought of anyting about an automobile. I don't know whether I put the brake on or put it in gear; anyway, it stopped on the edge. Our friend was absolutely horrified when he came out, and we were just hanging there."

Marjorie's approach to driving the gift car was the same approach she used later as she faced any new interest. She asked questions and she plunged in. In this case she called a friend and said, "Maybe you'd better tell me a few things about this car or something. The friend said we'd better go to the service station and get it filled up with gasoline, so she sat beside me, of course, and I drove it into the station and got it filled up with gasoline, and I did scrape one side. But that was the way my family treated me, you see. They expected me whenever anything came along to function with no instruction, to figure out for myself, or to ask someone who knew. And so that's the way I've functioned all along. I know I would have been much better many times if I had sought out someone who was knowledgeable, but I did things my own way,"

Marjorie's turning to her friend is another unvarying characteristic in her development. She treasures the thoughts and the relationships with friends. She says with conviction, "I have never lost a friend, and I still have as friends everyone I have ever been close to in my entire life."

High school over, Marjorie attended junior college for two years and then with a four-hundred-dollar scholarship from a group of university women she went to Rice, alone, on the train.

Was she afraid? "No, I didn't have any fear. In fact when they gave me this scholarship the women said, 'Now what are you going to do when this money runs out?' And I said, 'I'll get a job,' They said, 'Suppose you don't get a job?' And I said, 'But I will get a job.'"

She was already skilled in newspaper work and writing, and she did, in fact, soon have a job. For one brief period she was a cashier and she chuckles and describes it as the hardest job she has ever had. She remembers a day when she came up with a four-hundred-dollar shortage. She went to the auditor and said, "I don't know what I've done but I've done something," and she recalls they found a check for four hundred dollars that had slipped under a cash box. "That was the worst job, the hardest job ever. Teaching or writing a dissertation may have their moments, but deliver me from being a cashier!"

She married at nineteen and found herself functioning as a housewife who couldn't even slice bread. With abandon she told of having her math professor over for lunch and being unable to slice bread for sandwiches.

"Well, frankly," she says, "I didn't really try very hard to be domesticated. I was very interested in style, in decoration, and that kind of thing, but as far as cooking, well, I bought steak."

As the only married student on the campus she finished her bachelor's degree. Then followed the birth of her first child and what she calls her purity period. She attempted to become the perfect parent for her baby. "I became so good it was just unbearable," she says. "I left my newspaper friends entirely; I did not drink a drop. We never went out, except I went to church while my husband kept the baby. I must say, though," she adds, "that those were the Depression years and not many people were going out."

Two other children were born and Marjorie plunged again, this time into politics where she distinguished herself as the organizer of the first Young Republicans club, and eventually as the candidate for lieutenant governor of Texas. Calvin Coolidge was her cousin, and she felt that Texas suffered from not being a two-party state. She didn't win the election, but she gained the skill of being able to speak about anything as she says, "at the drop of a hat."

At about this time she reached a turning point in her life. She and her husband came to the breaking point of their marriage.

This period was filled with deep questioning and turmoil as Marjorie tried to understand herself and her marriage. She went to a psychologist, and she was deeply afraid he would tell her she should stay at home for her own good and the good of her family. She says, " I was scared to go because I felt I'd commit suicide if I just stayed at home. I literally was afraid of suicide and this, of course, created terrible conflict in me."

After much testing Marjorie was told that her marriage problems were a result of a mismatch of personalities. With this mental reassurance she withdrew from politics, and after a stimulating period of work creating art books for children, she decided to return to Rice for a master's degree.

This return was a radical departure at that time. No one had ever returned after a sixteen-year hiatus, and no one had ever returned after the age of thirty. But return she did, and completed her master's degree in philosophy.

The return to class was an exciting, thrilling experience for Marjorie. She says, "Actually, it was like being reborn when I went back to school, because apparently I have a real passion to learn if it's things I'm interested in. I would literally come out of class shaking with excitement at what I had heard and what I had learned."

Then followed a change to the University of Texas for a doctorate which she eventually earned in the field of literature.

There were always the practical ideas, the concepts running in tandem with academic work, and Marjorie submitted proposals for unique solutions to solving two problems with one action. "To solve one problem by the solution of another—there is a certain, beautiful economy about that. Of course, I feel that everything that is, is actually the divine consciousness unfolding itself to itself. Every idea as far as I'm concerned originates in that divine consciousness. And I feel that this is really a suitable way to solve one problem by the solution of the other."

She has thought long and creatively about everything from Sufism to the similarities between the Bedouins and the American cowboys. She has observed the change in attitude toward women, and she has formulated precise understandings. She says, "Financial independence is one of the first steps toward other kinds of independence for women, in my opinion, because many times women can't take certain steps about working, or further education, or travel unless they are independent enough to be able to pay for what it is they want. If they have to depend on male relatives who may be custodians of their money, then they simply can't do it unless they receive approval. Up until the present time that has been, of course, somewhat difficult to arrange many times."

She looks again at the thread which holds all women together, and she tries to give it a name. "Well, perhaps it is the solidarity of a shared problem and, of course, that is not to say that all women at the present time have to deal in the same way or with the identical problem. But it does mean that they are sisters and as human beings they have shared an historic role which has been delineated for them before they were born. They may, or may not, in their individual lives try to change it. We know that men have a kind of brotherly feeling when they meet each other, even if they have to meet without being able to speak in a language each can understand. There is a certain brotherliness there, and I'm sure that the same feeling of kinship applies to women.

"I think that the shared problem is actually one of coming to a satisfying and fair division of the responsibilities, benefits, and demands of life. It is not only family life, but the life of all human beings who live together and who must be fair to each other if anything constructive is to come about. I don't care whether it's a family, a school, a city, a nation, a country of many states, a continent, or the world. Problems have to be solved, and they have to be solved with equity and fairness because if they are not solved fairly, they're not solved."

Thought, experience, research, and conversation, these are all a part of the retirement of Dr. Marjorie McCorquodale. She says, "Although some people don't think so, life is really very long. And if you don't prepare for it by developing a love of literatire, art, music, and ideas in general, it can be a real bore."

She says that for her "now" is always her happiest time, and "now" is her most productive time. This is the attitude which creates life devoid of boredom, life filled with the vigor of interests always new, and always crying out to the explorer to come and investigate further.

13. Sharon Boswell

Faith Under Pressure
as Her Oldest Son Suffers from MD

"My faith is not in the doctors — it is in God. I believe that God works through doctors, but when you get a situation like this, where the doctors say there is just nothing they can do, then where can you turn?"

We anticipated anguish. We found serenity.

On the way to the interview at a fashionable address we talked of what it must mean to have a child who has been diagnosed as incurable and terminal. Since we both are mothers of two children we felt we could not only be sympathetic, but also empathetic with a mother who was in this situation — although we doubted our ability to comprehend what was in Sharon Boswell's mind at this moment of her life.

We drove into the exclusive neighborhood and walked slowly toward the house. I think we were both reluctant to face what lay ahead. Then Sharon opened the door. She was dressed in a pale beige silk shirt with matching pants and brown sandals. She showed us into a room filled with rich tapestry and antiques on burnished tile floors.

Sharon's story came quickly with assurance. She had a faith to reveal and a witness to share. Nothing else mattered, and regardless of the interview question, the answer always took a gracious but firm loop back to one central thought. Sharon had placed her child in the Lord's hands, and she had no reason for tension or dread. Everything was cared for; only peace lay ahead.

But how did Sharon arrive at this point? This was the question which waited to be answered.

Sharon took us directly to her experience of being born again and the peace which came from that experience. She began: "I was just going through life doing my own little thing and enjoying my art and creative writing. I thought the Lord was possibly opening up creative writing to me, but I didn't understand why, so I went to creative writing class. I really did learn in that class. I'd come home, I'd write things, then I'd discover they weren't very good, and I'd start all over, and write something else. But I could see that I was getting a little bit better each time I tried to put something down on paper.

"But a little after that, about a few years ago, my life changed. The doctors diagnosed my son John's problem as muscular dystrophy. I can only describe that by saying it was like someone had suddenly strapped a terrible burden to my back. You may have heard someone speak of being bent down with grief; that is what happened to me. I was weighted down with the heavy load of grief.

"I carried that around just like a two-ton pack on my back for about three weeks. I'd go to bed with it; it would be there, and I'd get up and it would still be there. I experienced terrible anguish. I have never had anyone real close to me die but it was that kind of grieving. I've never know grief like that before.

"The grief lasted two or three weeks. It got to the point where I just could not live with it anymore. And now I know that was really where God wanted me. I know you have probably noticed that until most people get their backs up against the wall they won't ask for God's help. They think they can do it. They can run their own lives. And really no one can.

"Finally I got to the point where I just couldn't live like that anymore. I just couldn't carry that burden and that was the turning point. I literally got down on my knees and turned things over to God as I said, 'God, you're just going to have to take this and take care of John,' I said. 'From now on John is yours; he's your child, because they have diagnosed him as incurable

Sharon Boswell is the wife of an attorney, a former model, and the mother of two sons, the elder of whom is suffering from muscular dystrophy. In spite of this condition Sharon is living days of contentment and peace because she has turned her son's condition over to God for healing.

and eventually terminal. I just can't take that. I really don't have the strength or the inner resources.' "

Sharon's voice was very calm as she spoke. She remembered the experience so vividly, and she especially remembered that she got on her knees to get help for John, but suddenly she found that she was looking at her own life.

"I found myself confessing all my sins, all the past sins in my life. And I realize now this is what the Holy Spirit wanted me to do. I did have to repent and truly be sorry for these things, so I could come into fellowship with God. I thought, *Well, I'll be here all night.* So I went through everything I could think of and I said, 'Lord, if I've forgotten anything, I really want you to remind me.'

"Then I went back to bed and in the middle of the night I had a dream. In the dream a voice said, 'You hold a grudge.' I thought a minute and I realized it was true. I can really think of the instances in my life that I had experienced where I had not forgiven people. I knew I was really going to need some help with this, so I said, 'Lord, you're just going to have to help me. I'm willing, will you help me? Help me forgive these people for these things.' And so He did.

"I kept on recalling instances of unforgiveness, and after a while I said, 'I know I'm still a long time away,' and the voice said, 'No, you're not.' It said, 'You're not five minutes away.' So that was my rebirth experience. I committed my life to Christ.

"So, through all of this I was actually born again. I had the true born-again experience. I thought all these years I was a Christian; as an adult I went to church every Sunday. I went to church where they taught very little from Scripture, and I thought I was probably as good as anyone else, and I was doing what I ought to be doing. I see now that God really let circumstances happen in my life to show me that I wasn't where he wanted me to be. Since then, since he took the burden and I committed my life to Christ, I really have total peace about

John. In fact, I have joy. I can go down the street pushing that wheelchair, and I feel like I'm just basking up there on a cloud. I feel this way all the time. I mean, almost all the time, every now and then Satan will come in and he'll try to destroy my peace."

Sharon's earlier years had not been filled with the kind of peace she described. She did not have a background of formal religious training, and neither her spiritual world nor her secular world was a world of peace.

She had vivid memories of an early childhood religious experience. She described it as she remembered it now. "One of the first things I recall is when I was about two or three. I'd ask my mother or dad every night if they would please sing 'Jesus Loves Me' to me, and they would sing that to me and rock me to sleep. I think that was the first religious experience in my life. I always look back on that, even though I wasn't really taken to church or Sunday School very often. Occasionally we'd go like a lot of people who go on Easter and Christmas, but I always look back to when I asked them every night to sing that song to me. I really looked forward to that, and at that time Jesus was so real to me."

Aside from this small island of security in a song, she remembers childhood as very insecure. "To me it was turmoil, and I reacted to the turmoil by withdrawing from it. I had a very difficult time coping with almost everything as I was growing up. In fact, probably my tolerance level for things that would come about during the day, ordinary things, was very low. I just usually couldn't cope with them at all. I would go to pieces. I had no strength then. I was just existing; it was very depressing."

She told of daydreaming of escaping her immediate environment, and writing was at times dreamed of as part of that escape. However, that too had problems. "I never had a great deal of drive. I always wanted to do those things, but I didn't have a comsuming drive to get these things done, and then I didn't have anyone who would encourage me to do them. Probably if I had some encourgement I would have gone ahead with a lot.

"I have one older brother; he's six years older, and I have a younger sister two-and-a-half years younger. I was always very much a loner and rather introverted, and my sister was just the opposite. So, in a way, I drew strength from her growing up since she was always able to do everything very well. She had a scholarship to Rice; she was really smart, and I always felt that everything I did took a little extra effort. It was a little bit harder for me to do things, but I have always been interested in creative writing; even when I was in high school I wrote things. I never tried to have them published, but when I was in the third grade I did a book reveiw and it was published. Such things have been a thread that has run through my life; I've always been interested in art, painting, and drawing. I always leaned in that direction."

Sharon's father had been a contractor-carpenter, and she remembers her mother as home-oriented, although she had worked outside the home during the Depression. Her mother liked to cook and sew, and in the years when there was less money she usually made clothes for the girls.

The years passed. Sharon finished high school and went to St. Thomas University where she majored in English. She said, "I had a priest there who really encouraged me with my writing; in fact, he told me that it was very good."

After graduation, Sharon worked as a model, but found that life too superficial to interest her. "That world just had no appeal to me; the jet set and all the care of make-up, dress, and hair just didn't mean anything to me. I have traveled, you know—we've been to Europe and that sort of thing, but it's not my thing to go around the world and buy mink or whatever. You know, that really doesn't turn me on.

"I also worked with a major industrial firm and I taught school for a year, but I never did see myself as a professional person working for the rest of my life."

Sharon married at twenty-six a young man who was working during the day and attending law school at night, and she received from him much encouragement in many areas of her life. She spoke of his help by saying, "He encouraged my writing, and he also encouraged me to get into activities and to have different outlooks. Right after we got married he would set aside fifteen minutes with me every night and act as a counselor. He tried to help me, but I really just couldn't unbottle all this stuff that had been in me for years. I just couldn't really share all those things that bothered me. So when something would come up that I just couldn't handle I'd call mother. She'd call the doctor, and he wanted to know why I was crying and why I was upset. She couldn't tell him and I couldn't tell her, and that just went on and on. I just couldn't cope with life at all."

With wonder Sharon looks back at her experiences as she searched for the kind of spiritual life that could give her peace—peace that would carry her through an experience which would be defeating to many people who consider themselves exceptionally strong. "I had gone down the aisle of the church and been baptized, but nobody ever told me anything. They never said to go home and read your Bible. They never explained salvation to me or any of those basics. So I just continued my life the way it was.

"Then, as I grew older, I didn't know that I needed to get into the Scriptures for myself; I didn't really have anyone there to tell me or train me. I got farther and farther away, and then I got off into a lot of things that I shouldn't have been into. I became interested in Eastern religions, in the occult which I think is one of the most dangerous things for people to get involved in, because when you try to go back and read the Scriptures, you really can't believe them.

"I got into palm reading and astrology, and there was a book about dream analysis. And after I read that book I was so filled with fear, I can't tell you how much fear I had. That's why I say that I can't warn anybody too stringently not to get into those things, because you may become obsessed with fear. I went through a period when I thought I was going to die all the time. I mentioned it to my husband, and he asked if I thought going to a psychiatrist would help. I said that I didn't really think so. I didn't know at that point what was causing my fear, growing up as I did without any background in Scriptures. I was really searching all these years, searching for God."

Sharon searched for God and grabbed what peace she could. She had found that she would be unable to have children so when she was thirty-three, she and her husband adopted John. Then about three-and-one-half years later they adopted Mark.

Sharon continued the story of her search. "At about this time I had been drawn more deeply into the occult, and by that I mean astrology and reading about the Buddhist religion and this type of thing. I got into yoga, just the exercise, but then they'd encourage me to meditate and do all these things. I guess about that time was when all the fear began to converge, and it just stayed with me. It began to increase to the point where I thought that something bad would happen to my family, that they would die, get sick, or be in an accident, and I was just constantly tormented.

"This fear went on for years. Finally it reached the point that I just didn't want to get out of bed in the morning. I thought, *I just cannot face another day.*"

We looked at Sharon's lovely surroundings and suggested that her recent life had been one of material enjoyment, but she waved our comments aside. "I was miserable in these surroundings because I had a void that was not filled, and I didn't know it. I was trying to fill it with all this other garbage, and I was becoming more and more in bondage and going into darkness, really."

We pressed her to consider that she had enjoyed artistic talent, leisure-time activities, physical sports such as tennis, and country-club fuctions. What part had these played in her adjustment to life and stress?

"I never cared anything about country clubs. We went to the usual parties, and even then I detested cocktail parties, and, of course, I detest them even more now. Oh, we would occasionally give dinner parties, but I've never felt really confident along those lines, as far as entertaining and getting everything all put together at the right time, and having it all come out right. I felt very insecure because I really didn't have that training growing up. What few dinners we have had we had catered, and we were fortunate enough that we could afford if and John didn't care. We didn't do it that often, and it just made it easier on me because I still wasn't coping well with the day-to-day realities. If I had to change on extra diaper that day or something, you know, I'd just go to pieces; I just couldn't cope with anything."

Since we had known Sharon earlier, during her period of great insecurity, we pointed out how completely she had concealed her fears, but it was hard for Sharon to believe this was true. "I had a friend of mine tell me that. I couldn't believe that she would think that because I was so insecure."

But the insecurity is gone now and has been gone for several years and Sharon agrees readily.

"I overcame it with God's help", she says, and the memory of the change is obviously still exciting to her. "I was rapidly going from bad to worse and I think it would have gotten much worse, but I don't think God would have allowed that. He allowed it to a certain point because he knew that I would be one that would turn to him when things got so bad because I already knew I didn't have any inner resources. Therapy wasn't the answer for me. I was really God-conscious all my life, and I guess really deep down I knew that was where my strength would lie without actually coming to grips with it before John's illness developed.

"I think from the beginning of my life I just basically was very aware of God and had a love for God, but I didn't know much about how to express it. I guess at some points in my life I was turned off by religion and that sort of thing. But, everything that's happened to me I know has been for a purpose, because I think I can warn people about the dangers of being involved in a lot of these things.

"I have a friend who not long ago went to a psychic, and I guess I can relate to her; she has had and still has trouble coping with things. And she has been depressed so she called and asked me about something with astrology, and I tried to turn her away from that. I hadn't talked to her in a while, and I heard that she had been seeing a psychic, and that's just not the answer. In my case it just filled me with fear and depression.

"That state of fear was the condition I was living in when I first got John's diagnosis. We had always known that there was something wrong with John, but we never could put our finger on it. We always felt that God had given us John for a purpose, although we didn't understand it. When we adopted the boys, deep down in both my husband and me, we had this knowing that it was right, even though at the time I was not born again.

"John was late sitting up and late walking. When he was very small, he always walked on his tiptoes and then he'd fall. He fell a lot, and he would usually keep a bump on his forehead from falling so much. You know how you sense something's wrong, but you just don't know. We took him to the doctors, and none of them really knew what we should do. One of them said John had some sort of brain dysfunction, but he never indicated anything like muscular dystrophy, So, it was not until about three years ago that they did a microbiopsy, and they determined that's what he had. So, it's a progressive thing. He walked until about two years ago, and then we had to put him in a wheelchair, but by that time it was almost as if we'd given him a ten speed bike because it had been such an effort for him to get up from the sofa to go across the room. He was delighted. Kids really accept or adapt to these things much more easily than adults do. I think John,

Sr., and I had a much harder time with this than John did.

"These first periods of being told that John had an incurable disease presented a communication problem for John, Sr., and me. I asked one doctor to look at John; I told him that he couldn't really get up off the floor; he had to get down on his hands and push up. The doctor said, 'Oh, that looks like dystrophy.' And that was the first inkling we had of what was wrong. The doctor made some appointments for us to see some specialists, and they confirmed it with their tests. But one of the hardest things for me was to come home and tell my husband what the doctor said, because he didn't want to believe it. He didn't want to accept it. And even when we put John in the hospital for a month or more John, Sr., would say, 'When we get a clean bill of health on John, we're going to do this or we're going to do that.' He wasn't accepting it even then.

"I think God compensates in some way with these children. I guess if we put most children in bed for a week they would just about tear up the room so they could get outside and start to play, but John isn't that way. He knows the situation, and he's basically very cheerful most of the time.

"He knows the name of the disease, but I have never gone beyond that because I don't believe it is necessary. I know that God has promised me he will be with John, and I know that God will heal John. I think that so many doctors just erase all hope. They'll say that you have cancer, or whatever it is, and you can't live more than six months or six weeks or whatever. So people believe it and they don't live beyond that point. So I am very strongly against a lot of discussion. I'm a person who can go through a medical book, and after I get through reading it I'll have all the diseases. I think most people are that way. And children are very impressionable."

Sharon described John's treatment plan. "He's been on an experimental drug program. I don't feel that he needs any further tests. And, as I said, my faith is not in the doctors—it's in

God. I believe that God works through doctors but when you get a situation like this, where the doctors say there is just nothing they can do, then where can you turn? The doctors just frankly told us there's not anything they can do. And they try to be honest with you. So I feed John the Scriptures; I don't feed him disease information. And I particularly feed him the Scriptures on healing. What God has provided through Jesus in healing."

John is now attending the public school so he will not become withdrawn from other children. He is now eleven, and he has the use of the upper part of his body although he can't straighten his legs to use his lower body effectively.

He particularly enjoys the family trips to New Mexico where the family goes to ski and to camp. Another camping trip is now in the early talking stages. He goes swimming about once a week, and he enjoys being outside with the other children where he watches them play ball.

We asked Sharon if it bothers John particularly that he can't enter into the games. "Oh, I don't think he notices it as much as I do. Kids will be kids, and they run off and leave him and that kind of thing. I think sometimes that probably bothers me more than it does him, but they don't do it to be mean—they just forget. They forget that he can't keep up with them."

We wondered how much communication Sharon had with other couples who have children in similar situations, but we found that this is not her source of encouragement. She told us that when she took John to the clinic she saw people who had similar diseases, but "as for a close friend, I don't know of anybody."

Sharon's peace and contentment are deeply rooted in her belief that God is caring for the entire situation and her specific belief is that God has promised healing for John. She told us of the nature of God's promise of healing.

"Healing just goes throughout the Bible and I started doing some research about what God had to say about it. There are so many promises in the Bible, and Jesus spent a good part of his time casting out demons and healing the sick. I did a lot of reading about that and I found that he never said 'No' to one person that came to him, so I prayed and I got an affirmative answer that God will heal John.

"I'm basing my faith on Scriptures of what God has to say about this. Many people still pray 'if it's God's will.' Well, I have researched the Bible well enough to know that it is God's will. He says it over and over again, and I can claim those promises, so I'm claiming them and I'm standing on God's word. Either God means what he says or he doesn't. So many people don't understand that, mainly because they haven't gotten to this point where they have to have him. I mean there's no other place to turn. God allowed me to see that there is healing in his Word, and I have taken John a number of times to be prayed for, and I just know in my heart that he will be healed and God has promised that to me.

"An interesting side issue of all this experience is the way it has altered my concept of the passage of time. I used to try to cram everything into the day. I'd make a list and I'd become very frustrated when I couldn't do all that I'd planned. I'd drive myself like a lot of people do, and I'd think I was really wasting my time; I should be doing this; I should be doing that, but I don't have that feeling anymore. So, right now I'm living in eternity; I've got all the time in the world, and I don't worry about it anymore. And that wasn't the way I lived before. The old way was total frustration.

"Now when I wake up in the morning I just praise God for my blessings, and I have found that when you remember to praise God, even in a situation that looks bad, he'll turn it all to your advantage. He'll make it work out right. I've seen that happen time and time again, and Romans 8:28 says 'and we know that all things work together for good to them that love God, to them who are the called according to his purpose'. So many people don't realize that God has their best interests at heart, and if He's allowing a situation as he allowed this with John he's doing it for our good. It's just a basic biblical principal if you read the book of Job and see what happens to that man and how, after all that suffering was over, God just gave him back so much more than he'd ever had before. I just look at it like God's my father so I know that my earthly father will look after me and how much more will he look after me."

"I don't have a feeling of being predestined in any situation. I believe that God gives us a choice. You could have a stack of lemons here, and you could just leave it that way, or you could made a lemon pie out of it. You've got your choice of what you'll do with your circumstances."

Sharon spoke of compensations which she feels God has given her, things which help her handle her life even in what appears from the outside to be a tremendously stressful situation. She agreed that some of her circumstances were good and that these were helpful in her contented life, and we were forced to agree that her relaxed appearance bore out what she was saying about contentment.

"Yes, I think God has really compensated with other things because our younger son loves school. He can hardly wait for the first day of school. Now how many children are that way? He does super in school. He's never known a stranger. He loves God and he's very attentive to spiritual things. My husband is very supportive, and God has given him executive ability. He has his own law firm. So, I really have everything going for me, so I think that God allows certain things to teach us the particular things we need. The things that I need to learn may not be the things that you need to learn, so your situation would be different from mine. I don't have stress. I really don't. Well, I think you can give all that over to the Lord, and in return he gives you the peace that you need and its's real. It's not wishful thinking. It just goes along with faith."

We recalled a story about Rosalynn Carter finding the burden of governor's wife so heavy that she said one night,

"I'm going to turn it over to you, Christ," and she did and she went to sleep. Sharon related quickly to this story by saying, "I'm sure she'd have to do just that, being the wife of the president now. I am always saying I just couldn't make it in a situation like that, but I said that so many times and when the situation would come up, then God was there with that special strength or whatever I needed, but he doesn't give it to us before we need it. So I've gotten to the point where I really should say, 'I couldn't do that without him,' because he'll give you what you need when you need it—but not before."

Sharon sees a bright future for her family. She looks into the future and says that happiness for her would be in being "wherever God puts us to serve him, and I really think that maybe my boys possibly will be in the ministry. I don't know, but if they were I'd be delighted. God may use them to minister without giving them a church, but I don't know that. In fact, I really feel that he will use both of them. I think especially after little John is healed that God will use him to encourage other people who have problems."

Sharon's faith was so strong it could be felt, but we wondered how Sharon reacted to the people who could neither experience nor understand her faith.

"I have an overwhelming love and a feeling of compassion, and I know that I don't have that capability for love naturally, so it has to be Christ working in me. I think I feel the way He'd look at us, with compassion. He doesn't put us down for our faults or our weaknesses, and always before I tended to do that. I at one time had a very critical nature. I was probably more critical of myself than anybody else, and that was one of the things that God delivered me from. So, I know that's one thing that I don't worry about anymore. He's literally delivered me from so many foibles, phobias, quirks, and unpleasant things inside me. He has given me a love, really, for all people. Now I don't sit back and say, 'Look, he's doing this or doing that, and I don't approve of that.' You know, I don't ever feel that way. I think perhaps if the Lord opens it up where I can share something of my own experience with other people I'll do it; otherwise, I'll just try to patiently show them as much love as I can."

She feels that the change in her life has been so dramatic it is apparent to all who know her. "I think my husband has been rather mystified. At one time he made a comment that I was completely different. I think the Lord just smoothed all the problems out, though. I think that it was such a new world for me, and it was so exciting that I could hardly handle it. I shared not long ago with a friend of mine—it was for me like coming out of a dark room into the light and never really knowing the light was there, and it's just been so fantastic.

"We are having so many days of happiness. I might mention that John's favorite time is when we turn the television off, get rid of all the distractions, go into the library, sit on the sofa, and we have, what he calls family time. We all share any ideas that we might have, or any problems that we have. Oh, he loves this! In fact, around Christmas we do this a lot; we have a fire in the fireplace and he calls it, family fire time. And so we all sit and just talk about anything that comes to our minds. His face just starts to glow. Oh, he loves this better than anything. And it's amazing some things he knows. He's soaking things in like a sponge. A lot of it comes from television and just being in contact with other children, and he likes to share all these things. And it really does something for his spirit. I am so grateful, and we have so many beautiful times together."

The evidence of the beautiful times together was on Sharon's face. Her faith was making of her days a constant island of peace in a situation which would have destroyed a person having less trust. We had learned from Sharon, and we went away realizing that our own stresses were indeed only the result of not understanding the source of peace inherent in faith. Sharon had tested the principle and her life was proving it's truth.

14. Dale Evans Rogers

Actress, Author, and Singer, Fighting Child Abuse

"You know, if you live to get to the top you often forget why you wanted to get there . . . but we have decided that the only way to really find ourselves is to lose ourselves in work for others."

We had planned to call her Mrs. Rogers. Yet when she stepped from the elevator we sang out, "Hello, Dale," as though we were old friends. Perhaps we have all ridden too many "Happy Trails" with her for us ever to be strangers again.

We planned to eat in quiet elegance with room service but actually ate in the bustling downstairs coffee shop with admirers interrupting to ask permission to snap her picture.

Both changes of plans were somehow right since our guest was Dale Evans Rogers, and Dale is totally at ease sharing encouragement with strangers, singing before thousands, or looking straight into the eyes of an interviewer while she occasionally reaches for a convenient hand and gives it a firm squeeze to make an effective point.

Dale is remembered by whole generations as the "Queen of the West" who rode and sang with Roy Rogers, "The King of the Cowboys," but Dale's life has been so much more than picturesque rides off into the sunset on the back of "Buttermilk."

She has been married three times. Of these marriages she describes the first two as total disasters. She has been a parent to nine children, three of whom died tragically. Robin, the only child born to both her and Roy, was buried in the afternoon of her second birthday in 1952.

In her book, *Angel Unaware,* Dale told of Robin's brief life as a victim of mongolism. In 1964 Debbie died tragically at twelve in a church bus crash and was remembered by Dale in *Dearest Debbie.* Sandy died at eighteen in 1965 while serving in Germany, the victim of a fellow soldier's dare.

Mixed with these periods of almost devastating sorrow there have been periods of high achievement.

Fan clubs around the world have enrolled some 15 million members to applaud Dale and Roy in 104 half-hour television films, the "GM Chevy Show," "The Andy Williams Show," as well as "Telephone Hour" performances and "Kraft Music Hall" appearances, to mention only a small part of the impressive list.

There were radio and movie performances in what Dale called "hayseed musicals." In one of those Roy is supposed to have told his co-star, "I think you're breaking some kind of record, Miss Evans; I've never seen so much sky between a horse and rider in my life."

There have been records and books. There have been television and radio shows, and there have been many appearances all over the country that blend into an unbroken line extending from the 1930s up to the present moment. These are still such a large part of Dale's life that she says she and Roy sometimes seem to have an "airport marriage" where they meet, kiss, and wave good-bye as one or the other goes off for an appearance.

But a new compulsion, or perhaps an old one reasserting itself, is pushing Dale on to do what she can to help with a problem which is breaking the heart of so many Americans, the child-abuse epidemic.

But before we talked about her work in helping to curb this ravaging blight, we wanted to know something of Dale herself, of her enduring spirit.

Through her tragedies and her successes, Dale Evans has developed a stability which precedes and surrounds her. We

Dale Evans Rogers has been successful in the world of movies, television, records, and books. Now with the same vigor she has faced other challenges, she faces from a Christian perspective the epidemic of child abuse.

asked about the development of stability in the pressured entertainment world, and Dale was firm in her answer that it did not come early to her.

"I never had this stability until I was 35 years old, unfortunately. I accepted Jesus Christ as my Savior when I was ten years old, and I should have made him Lord of my life at that time but I didn't. I hit dead-ends in my life, and I made many mistakes because I didn't put God first.

"But I finally learned that the things which will ultimately make you happy, most fulfilled, and most contented are from Him. I thought, for instance, that I had to be in the entertainment industry. He had given me a gift of composition and, in a sense, a gift of expression in writing, but I disobeyed my parents in my early teens, got married, and it was a complete disaster. My life was just a mess for years. And the more I did and the more I grasped for what I felt would make me happy in my life, the unhappier I became, and the more enmeshed I was in difficulty. And nothing was ever enough.

"I had such insecurity because I was deserted by my first husband, and my pride was hurt and, of course, pride is a terrible, terrible enemy to begin with. I was intent on striking back and making my mark. Probably if there had been Women's Lib I would have been in the middle of it at that time. And I'm so glad there wasn't, because that was a wrong attitude for me. Little did I realize that the only liberation, real liberation, is of the Spirit, and Christ brings that."

Dale had painted such a dark picture of her early rebellious years. We wondered if she now feels she could have been content if she had met Roy first, and experienced life as full-time wife and mother rather than as an entertainer.

"Well, I don't know. I can't really answer that. I just know that, from the time I was a very small girl, I liked to perform. I liked to recite, I liked to sing, and I would sing anywhere. As a little girl during World War I, I was very small but in railway stations my father said it used to embarrass him that I would sing at the drop of a hat, anybody's hat. So I guess I was born with that kind of temperament. But on the other hand that kind of temperament can be used in the home, as well to encourage children."

Dale speaks of her early home life with appreciation. "I've often said I wonder what in the world would have happened to me without a good, stable mother who is just as sound as—I'm not going to say 'as the dollar' because the dollar isn't very sound—but a very sound woman spiritually, morally, every way. However, she couldn't understand me very well, because I had a different temperament, and very early I wanted to be in the entertainment industry. I wanted to be an artist. I wanted to be a writer first—then I wanted to be a singer. I wanted to be an actress; I wanted to be a dancer—you name it. I had all kinds of things boiling around that I wanted to do. I think God gives us gifts or talents, and the marvelous thing to me is that he doesn't assemble them the same in any two people. And as far as aptitude, God gave that, you know, but what we're supposed to do is to let him channel it.

"I was rather precocious, and I had a great deal of self-will, and I never took too kindly to authority. I wanted to do it my way. I loved my mother devotedly, and my father, but there were just so many things to do. I had an opportunity possibly to go on the stage when I was eleven years old, dancing, of all things, 'The Charleston.' My church forbade me to dance, but I learned anyway because I liked it. I enjoyed it. And I wasn't even told about the stage opportunity for about six months, so I was pretty angry when I found out. But I understand perfectly now why my family had concern for me. The entertainment business has many pitfalls. It brings lots of joy and happiness to many people, but it is pretty much predicated on the ego. And that's a problem."

Dale feels that her early rebellion which led to marriage in her early teens was caused by both unavoidable situations and personal tendencies. Her childhood years were frustrating. She was mature for her years, and in the small town there was nothing to do; even school was unavailable.

"In the first place I was beyond my years, and I wasn't able to go to school early. At that time you had to be seven before you could enroll in the first grade and there was no kindergarten. And being the first grandchild I was taught how to read before I went to the first grade. I was an avid reader and I had an insatiable curiosity, and I wanted to go to school but I couldn't.

"My mother said I used to climb up in the tree in the back yard to watch the kids going into school. Then when we moved I went into the first grade and the teacher said, 'She doesn't belong in here.' I was seven, and they put me in the second grade, and they couldn't keep me busy so I went into the third grade. I'm no genius, but my family had worked with me, and I was thrown with children older than I chronologically, and I matured too rapidly. By the time I was ten years old I was more like 16, and I didn't enjoy girls my age because they seemed childish and this was a very unhealthy situation.

"I ran around with older kids, and then in the school there was a real wave of elopements of couples. I was going with a boy I really shouldn't have been dating. My parents saw that it was getting a little serious and they tried to stop me, so we eloped. It was horrible, just awful. Neither one of us was ready for marriage. Certainly I wasn't. I was as immature as anyone could be. And, you see, when you question whether anything could have stopped me from doing this, I don't really know. We're all different, we're all so different. But my mother's prayers never stopped. She never let go of me. She just believed that her daughter would come back. I finally, like the prodigal son or perhaps the prodigal daughter, came to myself."

Dale, in her writing, had mentioned a number of times when she felt God actually spoke to her so clearly it was like an audible voice. We asked if she thought such an experience were available to everyone?

"I think sometimes we hear God's voice in our hearts, and it's so strong that it's almost audible. I think that is what happened to me. One time I thought I heard his voice call my name, my given name, not my stage name. And it was very strong and I said, 'Lord is that you? Whatever you want, try to get my attention and let me know.' "

Dale feels great concern for young people today. "The world is constantly changing, but of course we all have to adapt. It would be so helpful if young people could realize that it doesn't matter what the framework is really, we each have to make our decisions. I think that the Lord guides today in our framework just as he did when he was on earth, and he has down through the subsequent centuries. I really and truly believe that this is the thing that makes me tick. This is the thing that keeps me going. Otherwise, I couldn't do what I do. I couldn't travel at my age. I've had sicknesses, illnesses, and a chronic condition, and there's just no way that I could do it without him."

And she is traveling and speaking. In short, she is doing what she does best. She is using every talent available to urge an awareness of the problem of child-abuse on communities, institutions, and individuals who can help in some way. She is facing a new challenge, not from a silver-studded saddle, but from a desk and a speaker's podium.

With Dr. Frank S. Mead, she has written a book on the subject, taking her title, *Hear the Children Crying*, from a poem by Elizabeth Barrett Browning. Mrs. Browning pled in the Victorian Age for the children who were being forced to work long hours in factories. That was a period when factory owners refused to shut down the machinery while the children attempted to clean it—with the result that children were maimed and killed. Dale points out in her book and speeches that the problem of child abuse today is still tragic, as she reminds readers that it has reached mammoth proportions in our society.

Dale sees the final answer to the battered-child situation as a religious one. She says, "There's no other ultimate answer. That is the last, final answer, because these people who batter children have to be changed, and psychiatry and psychology can really go only so far. It's similar to the situation with alcoholism and dope addiction. You can be helped, you can get off alcohol, and you can be given methadone for dope withdrawal, but in the final analysis that cannot keep you from going back to it. The desire within the person—whatever it is that clamors for drugs that give a sense of relief or euphoria—that has to be healed, and the emptiness has to be filled by God. The addict has to be given security within himself until he doesn't need that.

"I'm sure there are people who really question me about the book on that score, but I don't see that there is any other answer. The problem goes back to parents and their parents. The reason I say that is because a large majority of child abusers were abused as children, and it's like the Bible says, 'Train up a child in the way he should go: and when he is old, he will not depart from it' (Prov. 22:6). That can be the bad things as well as the good things. We have always had a tendency to think of that Scripture only from a positive side.

"They say that from one to five are the crucial years for a child—perhaps because what we learn then goes so deeply into the subconscious, it resides there and surfaces later. Those things are deep-seated. They're down there, and they trouble or bless later. And then, when these people who have been so abused grow up and have their own children and crises occur, they simply revert back to their parents' behavior. Perhaps in an argument with a child, or maybe in an economic privation, or maybe when they're ill, if they don't have a restraint, their early experience comes to the front and they do the same thing their parents did.

"There are different kinds of abuse such as mental abuse or berating a child and ridiculing a child until he has no self-worth whatsoever. Parents will say, 'You're never going to amount to anything; you'll never be anything. You're going to be just like your mother or like your uncle or like your father.' So then the child believes it, and so he ceases to strive or try, and then he's a dropout.

"Then there's a neglect when people won't pay any attention, and then the kids think they'll do whatever is necessary to get attention and then they do.

"You can see how so many of the things go back to early patterns of being ignored and neglected. There are so many early memories, those first things have to be healed. I believe many people need those inner healings. We've talking about the healing of the subsconscious, things down there that have never really been resolved and maybe that we can't remember. This problem has to be worked on from all the angles. It does—it does. But I think it is symptomatic of our turning away from God in our society that it is getting so prevalent and so violent."

Dale had mentioned that the child-abuse problem was symptomatic of our times, we asked her suggestions for caring for the children of working mothers in such a way that child abuse could be held to a minimum. We particularly asked about children being left in order that mothers could find fulfillment for their lives outside the home. She said, "I think one solution is to busy yourself with your talents in the child's school, in your church, in a woman's club, or service club, or whatever, where you are not expected to leave a small child for long hours. I'm talking about this period in a child's life from one to five years. There is time after that child gets to school for the mother to do more and our children are not at home terribly long.

"I think a woman should have a real hobby. I think she should start to develop something that she's intensely interested in against the time when the children are gone. And I think a woman should be preparing herself to work then if she wants to.

"There is always, however, a real problem in balancing the care of children and developing your own gifts. I think you're expected to use your gifts because if you don't use them they atrophy, but there are different ways of organizing your schedule to include your children in your total life.

"But I understand there are many factors; this is not a simplistic thing because we have so many needs and also stressful factors in our society. There is inflation, and many families can't make it if the woman doesn't work. But in a case like that I think that the sitter should be screened, and the parents need to be careful that someone who loves children cares for them. Someone needs to explain to the children that God loves them and that, although their mother is away from them, God is looking after them, and that after all is said and done God is their real parent.

"Then when the parents come home, the children should have golden time. Parents should have a good time with the children. Somehow that child is entitled to at least one of the days the parent has off from work. Too often the television replaces the parent and since television took over, we don't have the family comaraderie that we used to have. We need a wider view of fellowship with the children, and also of personal growth and satisfaction. This is very real to me, and I'm saying this because I'm a woman who had to work at seventeen to support a child.

"If it hadn't been for my mother who took care of my son, I'm sure he would not be the fine man he is today. But not everybody has that kind of mother, or maybe their mother is not able to provide care. So, we have to work with what we have. But some of the children can be taught to be independent in a sense. The whole situation has to be approached realistically."

In the research for her book on child abuse Dale had been surprised to discover that the average woman who was abusing a child was in her mid-twenties. She had thought it would be a younger and perhaps an unmarried mother. There was, of course, the problem of abuse where the boyfriend living in the home was abusing the child, sometimes with the sanction of the mother. Dale reacted with vehemence to the whole situation of the live-in friend.

"I think it's absurd. I think they're taking the icing without the cake, and too much icing is sickening. As far as I'm concerned, I haven't been any angel in my early life before I met Christ, but I never did that. I'm not patting myself on the back—I just happen never to have seen that you should give yourself to a man without any commitment on your part or his either. And where there's no commitment I don't see that there's any meaning to the relationship. I'm considered very old hat and square about this but that's alright."

We had expected Dale to say that her marriage to Roy had been a smooth one, but she surprised us by saying with a big laugh, "Not a smooth one, but a good one which is much better." She went on to tell us of the stresses on their marriage. "We've both been in the public eye, and we work together so closely, and we've had a lot of responsibility to the public, as well as our family, and it hasn't been easy. Roy and I have had disagreements, but we have shared a common faith. Had it not been for that, we never would have made it. For example, we had the child that was retarded and that separates lots of families. A lot of men particularly can't take it. They consider it an affront to their masculinity that they sired a child like that. I've received letters telling of husbands who just take off and leave the mothers with it, but Roy was so wonderful about it.

"If I never had anything else to love him for, it would be for two things, for the way he loved her and put his foot down when almost everyone that we knew except one minister told us that we should put her in an institution because she wasn't going to live very long. They all said that probably we would take too much time with her to the exclusion of the other children. Roy said, 'We will not do that; we will take her home and love her. And if we had not done it, *Angel Unaware* never would have been written. We would have missed the point entirely. The other thing I love him for is the marvelous son-in-law he was to my mother. He was so precious to her. There are very few men who will say, 'When is Mom coming? When is she coming back? I miss her.' And if I didn't have anything else to love him for, those two things would be enough."

Dale had spoken so much of her family, the six remaining children and their children. We asked how often they all got together, and we found that it had been about ten years since everyone had been home at the same time. "The family is so large now, and a child gets sick, and one of the families can't come. We do try to get as many as possible together for Thanksgiving, a picnic during the summer, and then about ten days before Christmas we get together for the Christmas tree, presents, and a big Mexican dinner. Sometimes they bring a dish, and sometimes I do it all."

I wanted to know whether Dale actually did any of the cooking or whether the "I" meant she supervised it.

Very quickly she said, "Yes, oh yes, I do the cooking. I love to cook."

She went on to tell of her years of housework. "I always took care of Robin on the nurse's day off and the time I was home. We had a nurse when I was working in movies with Roy. I couldn't do too much else then, but after we quit doing the series, I had the four younger children at home, and I did it all then. I had a woman that came in once a week and helped me. I did the laundry, and I did the darning of the boys' military pants; I did it all because I wanted to. I wanted to be a full-fledged mother, and I had the opportunity for about four years. I found that there's a great deal of reward in it. The four younger children and I had been very close. I love the others too, of course, but they were out and gone. I was working the whole time they were in junior high school and high school, and I almost killed myself trying to be a good mother. It's very,

very difficult, when you get up at 4:30 in the morning to make a location call doing Westerns and get home after dark, to have the strength and the will to look at homework papers or to talk with each child the way you should.

"It's very hard to ride the three horses of husband, children, and career and do all of them justice. Many times they split and you fall flat.

"But our sufficiency is of God and lately the thought of my own insufficiency has just eaten me alive, but all of a sudden this just washes over me, and I say, "The Lord is my strength.' "

Dale has spoken of many difficult times and many good ones. So, we asked her for the happiest event of her life. She recalled the publication of *Angel Unaware* and its becoming a best-seller as a very high point, but it was not because of pride in accomplishment; rather, it was because of the effect it had on the lives of mongoloid children, their emergence into the public.

"We did a theatre tour and people brought these children with Down's Syndrome (mongolism) backstage, and I had never seen one in public except one I saw in Central Park when I was in such a dilemma about writing the book. I couldn't decide whether it was God's will or just my wanting to get my hurt off my chest. That child helped me make my decision, and I feel I have had a part in the children coming into the light of day. I would say that has been the most rewarding event of my life.

"In a sense these children were invisible, and although they are retarded as far as considering the norm of intelligence, some of them, I think, have more wisdom than a lot of so-called normal people. Certainly they have more love. And the French people call those children 'those nearest the heart of God' because of their capacity to love and to give love."

Dale spoke always as she has lived, in a rapid hurry to get on to the next thing, and always she has rushed carrying others with her. As we left we were touched by a deep urgency within her, an urgency that leads her to help with whatever problem is near. She has lived richly but not smoothly, and there is no sign of slowdown.

She still has the goal of a good dramatic part in a picture, "but it would have to be a good, strong part that exalted God, that showed that right is might. And that's the only thing, really, that I have never done. When I did this book on child abuse, there was a script written for me, and I would have liked to do this two-hour special where I played an investigator for battered children. But nobody bought it—they couldn't see me in it."

So we came away with the feeling that where there are causes which need to be met, under the direction of God, Dale will be there—for as she had told us, that is what makes her "tick."

THE SUMMING UP

We had welcomed the early autumn with cool drinks and conversation in the suburbs. We had shivered in late autumn rains in small towns. We had battled winter's snow in city streets. And we had seen spring come in beside freshly cleaned backyard swimming pools.

And in each of these seasons and settings we had talked with women who were mastering some unusual aspects of life. Each of the women, whose ages varied from the mid-thirties to the mid-sixties, had told us how she had handled or was handling some life circumstance—whether it was a crisis such as illness, death, or divorce, or challenge such as becoming First Lady, building a second life, or retiring after a rewarding career.

We had interviewed and we had observed. After each visit we came away with new perceptions, new understandings, and new mental images of what life means to one woman of our time. Finally our remembrances and thoughts began to fall into place, and we saw the beginnings of patterns, as well as answers to some of the questions which had been in our minds from the start.

One of the most outstanding of these questions was: What are the traits these achieving women have in common with each other? Do they have common backgrounds? Do they think alike? Do they plan alike? We found that the answers to all of the questions were partially "yes" and partially "no." But there are some traits which they all seem to hold in common.

First, there was what Liz Carpenter called "elasticity." She felt that her upbringing—in a home with relatives and friends dropping in for an hour, a week, or perhaps a college semester—had contributed a flexibility which enabled her to adapt to new ideas, new residences, new jobs, and new circumstances in general. She spoke of growing up in a wider circle than an "in-house" type of family.

Mary McFadden used a different term for a similar experience. She spoke of "backing" into opportunities without predetermined goals, and of having the flexibility of mind to grasp those opportunities, turning them into personal success. Her view of elasticity emphasized an openness to new experiences and a readiness to move with the new idea or the new trend.

Connie Hill displayed the same adaptability. She had adapted early to change and travel in her pursuit of musical excellence, and when her way of life changed radically after her husband's death, she again adapted with a reaching out toward new musical and teaching experiences.

Marjorie McCorquodale displayed an unusual flexibility in her eagerness not to repeat past experiences in her retirement. She not only avoided the past working experiences but looked for and thrilled to a totally new experience in the world of the Arabian desert with its vast and starry sky. The safety of old experiences held no charm for her; stretching to fit the new challenge was more to her liking.

Dale Evans Rogers continues to meet and adapt to joys, tragedies, new career phases, and family traumas with a flexibility which denies her birthdays. She does not attempt to speak away the level of pain she has experienced. But like the proverbial rubber ball she bounds back each time to pick up her life and continue with a deepening level of awareness.

Joanne King Herring reveals a similar bouncing back after illness, divorce, and career changes; the pattern of resilience is repeated again. Liz's word "elasticity" can hardly be improved upon to describe the adaptation to changes of life directions which characterize most of the fourteen lives represented here. These women did not snap when the crisis or challenge came—instead they stretched and adapted until they could assume a new and viable shape.

Then there is a characteristic evident in these women which Mary McFadden described as a willingness to stand on the firing line. There is the willingness to take risks, the willingness to be vulnerable to failure. Several women responded to the question, "Were you afraid in that situation?" with a very blunt, "No, I didn't even think of being afraid" or "Yes, I was afraid, but I did not hesitate to try it."

Rosalynn Carter hit the campaign trail early with no guarantees of success and apparently felt a thrill in the challenge.

Evelyn Roberts spoke repeatedly of entering with her husband into mammoth new ventures, such as building a university or a hospital, and even though she knew the risks well, she was ready to appear before the camera or to stand before large audiences as she put her life and energies on the line.

There seemed to be a rejection of both mental and physical fear as these women approached their firing lines. There was not one interview in which the current threatening fears of being attacked, burglarized, or abused verbally became a topic of conversation. While the normal precautions of locked doors and safety alarms were in evidence at times, they seemed to be regarded matter-of-factly as necessary protection, but not as emotional burdens.

This attitude of lack of fear is evidenced as Jane Wyatt remembers her early attacks on the closed doors of Broadway producers as exciting rather than frightening.

The same lack of fear, or perhaps the control of fear, that empowered Rosalynn Carter to mount that first speaker's stand or enabled Lynda Jackson to take a thirteen-year-old transcript in hand to return to the college campus seemed typical of these women.

Beyond the elasticity and the willingness to stand on the firing line, there was a quality in most of these women which might best be called an explorer quality. They had a desire to explore those worlds with which they had no previous touch.

Dorothy Moore launched into uncharted areas of the world of crafts and skills and continues to do so with a rich verve. She is eager to master the world of minerals, Scuba diving, or bromiliad culture. She spoke of beginning work with metal sculpture because the welding equipment was present and unused in the garage. It was almost as though the presence of tools for skills commanded her to gain a new expertise. Even as the mountain must be scaled because it is there, for her the skill must be learned if the materials stand available.

Marjorie McCorquodale had thought long and precisely of the universe of thought and ideas, and she had accepted it as a personal call to explore.

Mary McFadden studied products and markets, and then did not hesitate to enter new areas of cloth design or perfume development.

Lynda Jackson saw herself as a student of new paths to serenity after her divorce, and she explored each path with a scientific eye, seeking out nuances of growth inherent in the divergent paths.

Along with the spirit of exploration, a number of the women expressed a feeling of mission. They felt that they had specific tasks which it was their unique responsibility to perform.

Ann Campbell expressed a conviction that, along with the blessing of the big family, there came what might be termed a "calling" to rear the children well. As Ann talked it was apparent that it was far more than a mere responsibility—it was the outworking of a divine plan.

Joanne Herring expressed the same sense of mission as she spoke of her work with the women's cottage factories of Pakistan.

Evelyn Roberts's sense of divine calling to the work of evangelism and development is almost a palpable quality. She speaks readily of worldwide plans, and she visualizes their fulfillment as miracles.

Ida Luttrell experienced a sense of mission, as well as a sense of universal understanding of the value of each human life, in the birth of her fourth child. And Sharon Boswell felt a similar sense of purpose and plan revealed in the lives of her two sons.

Dale Evans Rogers speaks repeatedly of the unfolding of her life, and to a greater or lesser degree most of the women expressed an awareness of a specific task, a specific way, a specific mission which was hers alone to accomplish.

There was an evident spirit of positive looking toward the future by these fourteen women. There was little regret expressed over past events, and where there was regret it was primarily over their own past inabilities to recognize the options which were open to them.

Dorothy Moore felt that her early horizons were limited by lack of travel and lack of vision of what was available to her.

Ann Campbell expressed a similar view of this situation by saying she could have gone to college, but that she did not realize college was a possibility for her until years later.

Dale Evans Rogers questioned whether the lack of early exposure to stimulating instructions and musical activities had forced her out into a competitive world before she was ready to face the temptations.

The positive side of early exposure to attitudes and opportunities is seen in Joanne Herring's early entrance into a world of social entertaining which continued to open wider until it became a large part of her life pattern.

The same early participation and exposure is seen in Connie Hill's entrance into musical training, a field which still provides a center for her life.

If practical observations for rearing daughters or sons is to be drawn from observing lives of these women, surely the value of wide exposure through early travel, instruction, and participation cannot be ignored. The world can be no larger than the individual perceives it to be, and perception comes from exposure.

As Ida Luttrell says of herself as she left for the university, "I was so green," she is undoubtedly giving expression to a widely shared feeling of lack of early experiences. However, the fact that Ida so early accepted the idea that she was college-bound indicates that her mother and father had made her aware of this option for her life. Here again is the positive picture of encouraging the daughters toward those opportunities outside the immediate environment.

Evelyn Roberts received encouragement from her grandmother to live up to her definition of a lady by excluding the use of any slang words. Her grandmother also encouraged her toward teaching as a highly acceptable career for a young woman, thereby pointing her toward a realistic option for her life.

Jane Wyatt knew from early childhood that she wanted to act, and her mother's position as drama critic, coupled with her own early attendance at the theater, doubtlessly made her entrance into the dramatic world smoother for her.

Among the interviewees over fifty years of age the statement was made repeatedly that only teaching and secretarial jobs had been suggested to them as possible vocations. This is a highly visible comment on changing patterns in society, since the below-forty group seemed to have escaped entirely the notion that career opportunities were so narrowly circumscribed.

Before beginning the interviews a number of knowledgeable people had suggested that we would find in able, achieving women a high identification with fathers and masculine figures in the home. However, in our group this did not appear to be a factor.

Rosalynn Carter was not untypical as she reflected that her mother had been a constant model for her life because of her courageous assuming of the role of breadwinner and guide for her children after the death of Rosalynn's father. Even now, when responsibilities and tensions are high at the White House, the First Lady looks back and finds encouragement in the thought that she has never been called upon to handle any situation as stressful as the one her widowed mother faced.

Several of the women seemed to have accepted college as a goal at an early age. There simply seemed to be a spirit in the home which urged them in that direction. Liz Carpenter spoke of a sense of historical achievement in her background which urged her toward preparation for accomplishment; Dorothy Moore spoke of her mother's direction toward education and Ida Luttrell told of both her parents often expressing conviction of the value of college.

Marjorie McCorquodale seemed to have had some inner knowledge that she would go to college, regardless of the lack of specific plans or visible funds. She speaks of a passion for learning which became increasingly evident to her as she progressed through advanced degrees. And, again, if we are questioning possible contributions to the lives of our children, perhaps we need to consider encouragement toward recognition of those dormant passions for specific areas of learning. Sharon Boswell spoke of the need for early encouragement of her creative writing.

Approximately half of the fourteen have completed traditional college degrees, with Marjorie McCorquodale holding the only Ph.D. In addition to the degrees, however, some have had several years of college, and others have pursued extensive programs of individual study.

Regardless of the exact program of study there was apparent in all a realization of the wide availability of knowledge, as well as the conviction that openness to learning was one of the true realities of life.

At least four of the women interrupted college plans for marriage, although among the four all had pursued further instruction or had definite plans for work in the future.

As a reflection of the effect our own historical era has on each of our actions, there was the implied thought that the timing of marriage had been a result of the prevailing philosophy of the day—that the individual step into marriage had been a result of the imitation of peers, that they had, as they often expressed it, "followed the herd" into marriage.

Dale Evans Rogers spoke of an epidemic of elopements following high school graduation, and she recalled her compulsion to follow the crowd. Ida Luttrell remembered the stigma of being an "old maid," a concept which has almost disappeared from our society in most areas.

Five of the fourteen women had been divorced, which is not too far from the national average. In most cases these women pointed, not to a dramatic incident or a staggering crisis as the reason for their divorce, but rather to a long period of growing apart after an early marriage. They felt that they had developed different interests and different lives from their marriage partners until their marriages no longer existed as a viable unit.

Several of these marriages were teenage marriages which had lasted until the wife's mid-thirties.

Three of the fourteen women were widowed, two by heart attacks of their husbands and one by a violent death. Each widow expressed adaptation to her new status without continuing grief or despair. Perhaps this was one reason for the evidence of vigor which we saw in these lives.

Liz Carpenter spoke about losing that feeling of being the most important person in another's life. Ann Campbell talked of grief washing over her at times now in a greater way than it had at the time of her husband's death. She attributed this lack of early grief to her responsibility to avoid grieving in the presence of her eleven children.

Connie Hill remembers the beauty of her marriage but shuns any continuing expressions of pity over her loss. With courage, she has moved away from past events. None of the three has remarried, and each has built a rewarding life around her interests.

As these women evaluated their life experiences it was interesting to note a recurring use of imagery. Connie Hill remembered her marriage as a perfect circle with no part missing. Ann Campbell spoke of her decision not to remarry by saying she thought of herself as "one" and of the children as the "other." A second husband would have been a third unit, and she had felt the melding of this third with the other two would not produce a harmonious whole.

Sharon Boswell thought of her rebirth experience as an emergence from a dark room into a light world which she had not known was there. Lynda Jackson saw her need to rearrange her furniture and outward life as an expression of her need for inner change.

Perhaps these and other images are evidence of a view of life which is essentially poetic, and maybe this poetic bent has added a strength of relaxation and perception to the lives in which it is present.

There were repeated statements by all the women of lessening of stress with the passage of years. Depending on the present age, each looked back to years when the children were younger, when they were all at home, or when they were all choosing careers as stressed times. Yet, in most cases, when asked for the one thing which brought them continuing joy, they answered, "my children."

The feeling of "family" was strong in lives as was the appreciation for and participation in religion. Sharon Boswell, Dale Evans Rogers, and Evelyn Roberts spoke of religion as the focal point of their lives. Just as surely Ida Luttrell spoke of her return to the church in a new way as she sought peace after the death of her sister. Rosalynn Carter spoke of the strength she received from shared Bible reading with the President. Although there was a varying intensity of conversation about religious interest, there was in each woman interviewed a statement of either a reliance on religion or an intent to pursue religious investigation.

There was a certain beauty of mind evident in each of these achieving women; complaint against the world in general was absent. In addition to a beauty of mind there was also a pronounced physical beauty and personal concern with appearance.

While fashion per se was of varying degrees of interest there seemed to be a high awareness of the force of beauty in homes as well as dress. We found ourselves discussing design with Mary McFadden, paintings with Connie Hill, fabrics with Joanne Herring, antiques with Sharon Boswell, boots with Evelyn Roberts, hats with Marjorie McCorquodale, dressmaking with Ann Campbell, glass with Ida Luttrell, portraits with Rosalynn Carter, book bindings with Lynda Jackson, autumn views with Liz Carpenter, special dishes with Dale Evans Rogers, the glories of ice cream with Jane Wyatt, and photography with Dorothy Moore.

We felt it was perhaps an evidence of a wider view of life which enabled each of these women to move verbally through so many areas of interest.

These varied interests and areas of awareness may have contributed to the general feeling of relaxation which we felt with each. While there were stresses both present and remembered, there was a positive aura around each. There was easy laughter at little things and an awareness of the small happy moment. Rosalynn Carter anticipated her 4:30 P.M. telephone call from the President, and Evelyn Roberts looked forward to the children home for the dinner she had cooked.

There was a spirit of joining forces with life rather than opposing it, and perhaps this in itself is one of the real reasons these women are achieving mastery over some difficult or challenging circumstance. They have placed their energies with life and not in opposition to it. They have discovered their own uniqueness and have committed that uniqueness to life.

Theirs is a positive affirmation of life's goodness as it appears to them. No one stated that life was either simple or easy, but each faced tomorrow with a courage which revealed . . .

A Kind of Splendor.